More Than A Coach **would not have been possible if not for the generosity of the following:**

Raymond L. Vaughn, Jr. and Suzanne S. Vaughn
Barry J. Mitchell and Lynn Vaughn Mitchell
Vaughn Development, LLC

Bob Burke
The Jay and Christi DeGeare Family
Oklahoma Christian University
Weldon & Cheryle Watson

Harold "Hal" & Mary Beth Ballou
Richard & Ada Blankenship
Randall & Barbara Heath
J. Terry & Martha Johnson
Stafford & Jo Anne North
Harry & Brenda Patterson
Dr. & Mrs. John Scroggins
Clint & Sheridan Vaughn
Lawson & Erin Vaughn
Kathy Wright

nor and title page images courtesy
lahoma Historical Society.

OKLAHOMA TRACKMAKER SERIES

Raymond L. Vaughn, Jr.

MORE THAN A COACH:

Remembering the Life of Ray Vaughn

Foreword by J. Terry Johnson

Series Editor: Gini Moore Campbell

OKLAHOMA HALL *of* FAME
OKLAHOMA HERITAGE ASSOCIATION PUBLISHING

OKLAHOMA HALL *of* FAME

BOARD OF DIRECTORS

DEDICATION

I would like to dedicate this book to my family—my wife Suzanne, children Christi and her husband Jay, Lawson and his wife Erin, and Clint and his wife Sheridan, my grandchildren Jakob, Taylor, Greyson, Lydia, Liam, Hudson, Garrett, Austin, and Brooklyn, and my sister Lynn and her husband Barry—and to all those who had the good fortune of knowing Coach Ray Vaughn.

CONTENTS

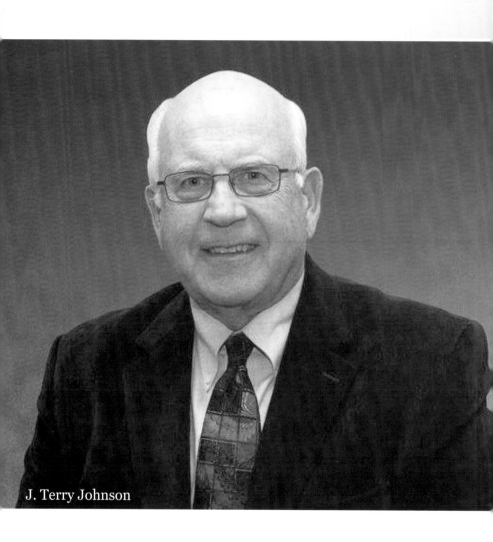

J. Terry Johnson

FOREWORD

"Coach Vaughn" was already a living legend by the time I arrived on the Oklahoma Christian College campus in the fall of 1961. Transferring from Southern Methodist University where I had lettered on the freshman baseball team, I was eager to extend my college career as a "walk-on" sophomore. The truth be told, all members of the Eagle baseball team in those years were walk-ons unless they happened to have a basketball scholarship that required them to participate in one of the spring sports. Track and basketball were the two premier programs and both were coached by the man who was loved universally by students and faculty alike – Coach Ray Vaughn.

In a matter of three years, Coach Vaughn had transitioned from being a celebrated high school coach at Capitol Hill to become a well-regarded college coach, capable of recruiting exceptional athletes, conditioning them for competition, and bringing out their best efforts on the field of play. He stood tall among his peers.

Decades have passed, but I can still recall the familiar image of Ray Vaughn driving his pick-up truck along the roads near campus, timing the cross-country team members as they labored through their conditioning routes. Coach Vaughn poked his head out the open driver's window, shouting time splits to the runners, while his black dog Tallahassee, a constant companion, stuck his head out the passenger's window. The two were inseparable. One day while traveling with me on a business trip, Dr. James O. Baird, the founding academic dean and second president of Central Christian College, shed some light on the legacy of Ray Vaughn. "Hiring Ray was a critical factor in both the college's transition from Bartlesville to Oklahoma City, and its emergence as a credible four-year institution of higher learning," Baird confided. "It would have taken many more years to establish ourselves as a senior college without a viable inter-collegiate athletic program. From the outset, he put winning teams on the track and basketball court, calling on the faculty to keep pace in their efforts to develop the college's academic standing."

Sports enthusiasts who knew Ray Vaughn through the articles in the newspaper were acquainted with his professional successes, but they could hardly imagine what he meant to the young men who came under his tutelage. He inspired these athletes to become honorable citizens, loving husbands and fathers, faithful servants of the Lord Jesus Christ, and decent human beings who would bring honor to their family names. He was the consummate mentor, interested in all facets of the student-athletes' lives.

Coach Vaughn married well. His wife Sue was his best cheerleader. In the spring of my sophomore year, I enrolled in Sue Vaughn's speech course. Her style was one of her own choosing. Let me just say, before there was Erma Bombeck, there was Sue Vaughn.

Sue Vaughn was an accomplished leader in her own right, teaching at the college level and providing guidance for the Oklahoma Christian Women's Association, an organization that has raised thousands of dollars for numerous campus projects. She adored her husband, always speaking of him affectionately as "Coach." As a couple, they opened their home generously to students, feeding them Sunday night meals that often featured Sue's cinnamon rolls for dessert.

This biography of Raymond Lawson Vaughn, written by his son Ray Vaughn, Jr., is a tribute to the genius and effectiveness of a humble man. Born and raised in rural Oklahoma, open to educational opportunities and a professional career, Ray Vaughn developed vital leadership skills while serving his country in the United States Navy during World War II. He was proud of his family, his country, and his Oklahoma roots. As you read the stories of those whose lives were influenced by this amazing man, you will come to appreciate the core values of the man they called "Coach."

J. Terry Johnson
President, Oklahoma Christian University
1974-1995

Coach Ray Vaughn

PREFACE

Coach Raymond L. Vaughn enjoyed a very successful and sometimes exciting career doing what he loved with people he cherished and who loved him, leaving a legacy worthy of this study of his life. Raymond Lawson Vaughn was a giant of a man although he stood a mere 5' 11" tall. It wasn't so much his size that made him big as it was what he did. He exuded confidence yet carried himself with an openness that put even strangers at ease, making them feel comfortable even if talking to him for the first time. Perhaps it was his upbringing, being the youngest child in the family, or perhaps his years in the military or those teaching high school and college, or the combination thereof that made him a genuinely likeable person.

By man's standards he wasn't on this earth long, just 63 years. I was 32 when he died. Yet, because of who he was and the public life he led, I am blessed with a written record with which to supplement my memories. This book is a combination of both.

Ray, Sr., as a lot of his friends called him, had a humble origin but actually made it to the world stage. He didn't talk much about his life or accomplishments, making it all the more meaningful to his family and to those that he influenced to document what they were. The first three chapters of this book are based on discoverable facts about his childhood, archival documents at Harding University and elsewhere and detailed military records provided by the United States Navy. From chapter four, and following, I was blessed to witness, in part, his career first hand and to learn from him how to be a strong Christian, husband, father and leader.

Education is one of those professions in which an individual, such as Coach Vaughn, has the opportunity to interact with a number of people. As a teacher, literally thousands of students come through your classes in a career. You have a relatively short period of time in which to share your thoughts, advice, and training with them before they move on to someone or somewhere else.

The following accounts of his students, athletes, friends, and family give us insight into his teaching and mentoring skills and leave us with an impression of what he was like and what his direction meant to those that were subject to his oversight and influence. I'm sure there are many other examples that could have been included; however, those that I was privileged to gather and include herein tell us about the kind of man Coach Vaughn was and how those that knew him were blessed by their experience.

Raymond L. Vaughn, Jr.

2016

ACKNOWLEDGMENTS

When I decided to undertake the writing of my father's biography I first met with an acquaintance of mine from both my radio broadcasting and law profession days by the name of Bob Burke. Bob has produced more biographies about Oklahomans than anyone else. He encouraged me to proceed and offered to help with any technical advice that I might need. Among his advice was that I consider working with Gini Moore Campbell, vice president of the Oklahoma Hall of Fame. I have done so and it has been a pleasure. Gini has published a number of books and brings the technical advice and experience needed by a first-time author such as myself. My thanks also to Mr. Jeff Briley, deputy director of the Oklahoma History Center, along with Laura Martin who heads up the research library, who were able to provide a substantial amount of information and photographs regarding my family and my father.

There wasn't a great deal of information available regarding Raymond Vaughn's childhood in Washita County. Sources included stories from family members and personal memories. Old family photographs, which were few but precious, shed light on at least how the family looked and how they lived.

Washita County has its own historical society, which longtime native and local historian Wayne Booth, age 92 at the time I was consulting with him, staffed on a weekly basis. Wayne has actually written his own book about Washita County's early days entitled *Images of America-Washita County*, which was very helpful.

A booklet entitled *Cordell's Christian College—A History* by Norman L. Parks provided a good synopsis of the founding and history of Oklahoma's first Christian college.

Charlotte Dodson, who founded Dodson's Cafeteria in south Oklahoma City, along with her husband Joe, having been born and raised in Cordell, provided an insightful description of being a child in Washita County during the Depression.

Leah Walton of the Harding University Office of Alumni and Family Relations, and Jean Waldrop, director of the Brackett Library, were very kind and responsive in providing me with digitized copies of the Harding College *Petit Jean* Yearbook and the Harding College campus newspaper, *The Bison*. These documents were a treasure trove of both written accounts as well as photographic evidence of his collegiate exploits and athletic successes. My wife and I also visited the campus during the compilation of this book where Cindy Hunter, assistant to the president, helped us obtain the photographs of Coach Vaughn's induction into the Harding University Athletic Hall of Fame.

Like many of our soldiers and sailors in World War II, Coach Vaughn spent almost no time talking about his military career. For a very nominal fee, the United States Navy, or any other branch of the service, will provide individuals with copies of their families' military records upon request. The information I received included an enlistment photo and numerous copies of orders, assignments, and reports. I extend my gratitude to the United States Navy for the record they kept of my father's experiences while in the service to his country, and their readily providing me with such upon request.

Coach Vaughn was blessed by being able to serve two fine educational institutions during his lifetime. The first was Capitol Hill High School, where as a thirty-year old college graduate he was given the opportunity to build a state high school championship track and field team and ultimately serve as the athletic director. He also had the opportunity to participate in the construction of an innovative and iconic "round field house", the first of its kind, in Oklahoma.

Longtime Oklahoma City educator, administrator, and Capitol Hill High School (CHHS) graduate, and ultimately the school's principal, Ray Thompson was very helpful in providing information on Coach Vaughn's early coaching and teaching career. Former CHHS students and athletes including Oklahoma City businessman Dick Soergel, Don Ladd, Capitol Hill Baptist Minister Jim White, professional basketball player Hub Reed, Dr. J. Don Harris, State Champion sprinter Frank Taylor, runner and later CHHS track coach Tom Hibbitts, and John Doughty all contributed valuable insight. My thanks goes also to the *Capitol Hill Beacon* Newspaper for the many articles and feature stories on both the school and Coach Vaughn.

I am also indebted to Mrs. Gail Payne who, along with her husband

Bill, gave me my start in broadcasting and provided the photos from KWHP Radio.

What else can I say about Olympic Gold Medalist, J.W. Mashburn? He graciously sat with me at least four or five times to share or review information and photographs about his storied career which really had its start at Capitol Hill High School with Coach Vaughn. My sincere thanks and appreciation to him.

Having already successfully built the track and field program at Capitol Hill High School from the ground up, Coach Vaughn was the perfect candidate to do so again at what is today Oklahoma Christian University. The school's *Aerie* annual yearbook was of great assistance in documenting the development of the entire athletic program from basketball to track and field and beyond.

Oklahoma Christian men's basketball coach Frank Davis added valuable third-party accounts that supplemented personal interviews with such early day standouts as long jumper Richard "Dickie" Gray, quarter-milers Harold "Hal" Ballou and Forrest Reed, decathlon star Gary Hill, thrower Jim Neugent, race walker Dale Paas, and four-time All-American distance runner Mike Herndon.

Special mention must be made regarding the personal assistance and encouragement given to me by my childhood friend, brother in Christ, and successor to my father as the Oklahoma Christian University head track and field coach, Randy Heath, who spent hours documenting and detailing the performances of the athletes set forth herein.

Jeff Bennett's story of athletic achievement from Vinita, Oklahoma to the stage of the International Olympic Games in Munich, Germany seems rather implausible in and of itself.

My thanks to him for helping me, on many occasions, whether it be personal interviews or the sharing of valuable mementos and photographs. Jeff's story will encourage all who long to follow in his footsteps and see how far their talents and opportunities will take them. My thanks to former miler and dean of the Oklahoma Christian University Bible Department Lynn McMillon, cousin, educator and Evangelist Bobby Vaughn, Dr. Robert Watson, Evangelist Jim White, Doy and Pat Burchel, Coach Frank Davis, businessmen Dave Smith and Gary Hill, and the best sibling a guy could ask for, my sister, Dr. Lynn Vaughn Mitchell for their memories of Coach Vaughn.

Finally, a special thanks to my wife of close to fifty years, Suzanne Steele Vaughn, who tolerated and even encouraged my late nights and weekends spent in researching and writing this biography about a man we both loved and respected and for her expertise and advice regarding the Sue Vaughn Cinnamon Roll Recipe, which she can execute perfectly.

To all of these mentioned above, I owe a debt of deep gratitude.

Raymond L. Vaughn, Jr.

2016

The Vaughn Brothers in Cordell, Oklahoma. Raymond L. Vaughn is far right.

CHAPTER ONE

Growing Up in Washita County, Oklahoma

Raymond Lawson Vaughn was born on the 21st day of September, 1916 to William Thomas "W.T." Vaughn and Bessie L. Coons Vaughn in a very inauspicious farm house a few miles southwest of Cordell, Oklahoma, the county seat of Washita County. The fifth of five children in the family and the fourth of four sons, Raymond would grow up fast trying to keep up with his older siblings and performing the daily chores on the wheat and dairy farm that had to support a family of seven.

W.T. Vaughn was born in Kentucky on the 7th of July, 1881. He finished high school in Paragould, Arkansas before returning to Kentucky where he attended college in Bowling Green. W.T.'s first wife, Essie Caroline McLauchlin, of Green County, Arkansas bore a daughter, Jewell Belle Vaughn, born on July 31, 1905. Essie died four years later at the age of 28. The following year Vaughn married Bessie L.

W.T. Vaughn and Bessie L. Coons Vaughn were the proud parents of five—daughter Jewell Belle Vaughn from Vaughn's first marriage and sons William Thomas Vaughn, Jr., David Freeman Vaughn, Paul Harding Vaughn, and Raymond Lawson Vaughn.

Coons on August 9, 1910. Bessie bore four sons into the Vaughn family: William Thomas "Jack" Vaughn, Jr. born on September 10, 1911; David

Raymond Lawson Vaughn with his dog and cat.

Freeman Vaughn born on January 4, 1913; Paul Harding Vaughn born on October 27, 1914; and Raymond Lawson Vaughn born on September 21, 1916.

W.T. Vaughn was a farmer-rancher, teacher, school administrator, and church of Christ preacher. As time passed, Jewell Vaughn married Vern Stafford and lived in Amarillo, Texas and Tulsa, Oklahoma where she and her husband owned and operated motels. Jack Vaughn, the eldest son who lived near Tecumseh, Oklahoma was also a farmer-rancher. Freeman Vaughn, who lived in the Tulsa, Oklahoma and Rogers, Arkansas areas was a church of Christ preacher and was at one time the director of the Turley Children's Home in Turley, Oklahoma. Paul Vaughn spent his career in the Navy and retired in California. Raymond Vaughn was a lifelong coach and athletic director, serving in both capacities at Capitol Hill High School and ultimately Oklahoma Christian University.

The first "run" that settled such central Oklahoma towns as Guthrie and Oklahoma City and made history worldwide occurred on April 22, 1889. The second "run" occurred almost three years later on April 19, 1892 and established County "H", later to be known as Washita County.

Washita County, although relatively new geographically, already had developed a rather interesting and diverse reputation. Originally the home of the Cheyenne-Arapahoe Indian Reservation, Indian Agent John H. Seger became the first white settler to live on reservation property when he made his home on Cobb Creek in what would become Colony, the first town settled in Washita County.

Indian Agent John H. Seger settled the town of Colony. The first town in Washita County, the Colony Post Office was established on January 8, 1896.

Shortly thereafter, in 1889, Seger recruited 500 Native Americans to join him at his settlement. Washita County Historian Wayne Booth recalls the story: "The Sunday morning before they started their journey from Darlington, Seger read the Bible story of the River Jordan and compared their journey to the Bible story. When the group came to the Canadian River, about 40 miles east of Colony, they discarded their native garb, bathed in the river as a symbol of washing away their old life, and dressed in new white men's clothes that the government furnished. They completed the journey and established the town of Colony, which still exists today."

The county enjoyed a rich agricultural and ranching economy based primarily on cotton, wheat, and cattle. By 1905 the Hughes Ranch had become a 20,000-acre spread in the southeastern quadrant of the county. The Washita River ran through the ranch making it an attractive and productive source of revenue; however, there was a darker side. "The Hughes Ranch is not remembered as an agricultural ranch, but was

The Vaughn brothers in a cart pulled by a goat. Raymond is far right with his eyes closed.

well known as a hideout for outlaws. Many were shot at, and some hit, as they attempted an arrest at the ranch for outlaws such as Red Buck, Cole Younger, Ben Casey, Al Jennings, the Daltons, and others."

With their only sister being six years older than the oldest brother, and there being only a five-year difference between the oldest and youngest boys, it was natural that the brothers spent a lot of time together growing up. Most boys have a natural affinity to almost any type of sport, especially when teamwork and competition are involved.

That combination led to an event that Raymond would remember the rest of his life. It is common while playing baseball amongst boys of different ages, that the oldest and biggest of the clan assume the pitching duties. Likewise, no one really wants to be the catcher, therefore those duties often fell to the youngest and smallest participant.

One day as the boys were playing baseball, Jack was pitching and Raymond was catching. The batter managed to hit an infield pop-up directly between home plate and the pitcher's mound. As both Jack and Raymond rushed to make the out, focusing intently on the ball, they collided with the taller Jack's elbow making contact with the shorter Raymond's mouth. The result was the loss of all four of Raymond's permanent upper teeth. Later in life, Raymond had to actually obtain a waiver to enter the United States Navy as a result of his having false teeth. He never complained about this disability and it often provided a surprising method of scaring small children, and sometimes adults.

CORDELL CHRISTIAN COLLEGE

Although it is unclear how W. T. Vaughn arrived in Cordell, Oklahoma, due to the fact that he remarried in Oklahoma in 1910 following his first wife's death, it is plausible that he was recruited to either preach at the Cordell Church of Christ, which was founded in 1894, or perhaps as an administrator/teacher at the still fledgling Cordell Christian College which had its beginnings in 1907. He served as both the full-time pulpit evangelist at the church and also as the headmaster of the elementary school attached to the college.

In 1994, the 4th & College Church of Christ in Cordell published a

W.T. Vaughn, right middle row, and his wife Bessie, middle row seated left, with a class of grammar school students in 1926. Raymond Vaughn, age 10 and apparently not too excited about having to pose for the class photograph, sits on W.T.'s right.

commemorative booklet entitled *Cordell's Christian College–A History* by Norman L. Parks in conjunction with the church's centennial celebration. Parks reported that John Nelson "J.N." Armstrong had begun a decade of service to the college in the fall of 1908. Parks further reported under the heading "Added Faculty In 1910" that Armstrong "employed W.T. Vaughn to head the grammar school. He was a successful preacher who made Cordell his permanent home and became a leading influence in the community".

Cordell Christian College, known during its nearly two decades of operation as Western Oklahoma Christian College and Oklahoma Christian College, enjoyed periods of growth and success as well as periods of uncertainty and despair. Much of that had to do with leadership.

Armstrong went on to become the first president of Harding University in Searcy, Arkansas, a sister university that continued to thrive.

As Oklahoma Christian College in Cordell prepared to open classes for its 20th year in September of 1929, the post-war depression already had hit the agriculture industry and many cotton growers were struggling. The ultimate stock market crash in November of 1929 created an economic crisis unlike

The main building and women's dormitory at Cordell Christian College.

anything these Americans had faced before and private higher education was not immune.

Parks credits the schools ultimate closure following the 1930-1931 school year to not only a poor economy, but an "unfortunate" selection of a new president to head the school who was unable to generate the support to sustain it. Following commencement exercises in 1931 there was uncertainty as to whether or not the school would be able to open in the fall.

"A sizeable number of church of Christ members at Cordell were unwilling to see the institution die without making an effort to save it. They found their spokesman and leader in W.T. Vaughn," Parks stated in the history.

In regard to W. T. Vaughn's contributions, Parks said "W.T.

The Washita County Courthouse in Cordell was the work of
Solomon Layton prior to designing the Oklahoma State Capitol.

Vaughn was known to more students during the life of the college than any other man, for he sent his children to the college and addressed student assemblies year after year. Moreover, he sent many young people he had baptized to its doors. He deserves to be remembered for his heroic efforts to save the college during the 1931-1932 period."

There is no doubt that Cordell Christian College satisfied a valuable need in higher education at that time, just as its successor, Oklahoma Christian University in Oklahoma City, does today. To understand the relationship between the schools, one only has to look at the prominent building with the tall steeple seen from the entrance of Oklahoma Christian University. There hangs the bell from the bell tower of Cordell Christian College which still chimes today over the classes where students receive a first-rate Christian education in Oklahoma City.

CORDELL DURING THE DEPRESSION

Although Cordell was considered one of the largest and fastest growing cities in western Oklahoma at the time, it was certainly not immune from the economic collapse and ultimate depression to follow. By statehood, in 1907, the population of Washita County stood at just over 22,000; however, it had climbed to almost 30,000 by the time the depression swept through the state. According to the most recent census, in 2010 Washita County's official population was 11,629 with 3,433 of those individuals living in the Cordell zip code.

Joe and Charlotte Dodson, the well-known and beloved couple who fed many south Oklahoma City residents through their Dodson's Cafeteria for almost fifty years, were both born in Cordell just prior to the depression.

Charlotte's father, Les Day, was a linotype operator for the local *Cordell Beacon* Newspaper, earning $25 per month. Because of his training and skills his job was reasonably secure, while

Joe and Charlotte Dodson, founders of Dodson's Cafeteria. *Courtesy of Joe and Charlotte Dodson.*

many in the farming and ranching business had to make ends meet by selling eggs and cream to the local markets.

Joe's family was "wealthy" according to Charlotte. Joe's grandfather, John Austin Dodson, was a well-known state legislator from the area and Joe's parents already had established themselves in the restaurant and department store business.

While Charlotte describes the Depression years as "horrible", she hastens to add that both she and Joe loved growing up in Cordell. She recalled that on Saturday nights the farming families would come to town to shop and even take in a movie at the local theatre on the town square and that "everybody" was in church the next morning.

Raymond Vaughn was thirteen years old when the stock market crashed. By the end of the Depression, almost four years later, the Christian college in Cordell had closed and Raymond was finishing the eleventh grade at Cordell High School where he would later graduate in the spring of 1934.

In addition to "pulling his weight" around the farm, Raymond excelled in education and athletics. He played basketball and baseball for the Cordell "Blue Devils", an interesting mascot for a preacher's son. His exposure to sports developed and demonstrated not only his talent to participate as an athlete, which he would do until his untimely death, but also his ability to coach others and help them achieve feats beyond even their own expectations. Raymond Vaughn's life centered on his love of God, his family, education, public service, and certainly athletics, both his own pursuits and his encouragement of others in theirs.

Raymond L. Vaughn, standing right, while attending Harding College.

CHAPTER TWO

Captain of the Harding College Basketball Team

In the fall of 1934, Raymond Vaughn and his older brother Paul enrolled in the freshmen class of Harding College in Morrilton, Arkansas. The merger of Arkansas Christian and Harper colleges resulted in Harding College being located in Morrilton on the former Arkansas Christian College campus prior to its relocation to Searcy, Arkansas.

How did the Vaughn boys get from Cordell to Harding College? Years earlier, the Potter Bible College was founded in Bowling Green, Kentucky by James A. Harding. Harding, along with his daughter Woodson Harding and her husband, J.N. Armstrong, later relocated the college to Odessa, Missouri where Armstrong took over the presidency of

PAUL VAUGHN
Rocky, Oklahoma

LOIS SELF
Quail, Texas

CLYDE E. JAMES
Judsonia

HELEN WALLACE
Wardell, Missouri

RAYMOND VAUGHN
Rocky, Oklahoma

GEORGIA PRUETT
Searcy

Harding College's freshmen class in the 1935 *Petit Jean* Yearbook included brothers Paul and Raymond Vaughn from Rocky, Oklahoma.

the institution which was renamed the Western Bible and Literary College.

J.N. Armstrong, who previously had served as president of Cordell Christian College, became the first president of Harding College in Searcy, Arkansas.

After two years and a bout with poor health, Armstrong resigned as president. However, in 1908 he accepted the presidency of the recently founded Cordell Christian College and in 1910 hired W.T. Vaughn as the headmaster of the academy attached to the college. Armstrong remained at the helm of Cordell Christian until its temporary closure in 1918 due to World War I.

When Cordell Christian shut down, a number of the administrators and faculty, including Armstrong, became affiliated with the recently established Harper College in Harper, Kansas where their work continued until 1924. At that time, Harper College was consolidated with Arkansas Christian College in Morrilton, Arkansas and the resulting institution was renamed Harding College in honor of James A. Harding with J.N. Armstrong, his son-in-law, serving as the new school's first president.

It is certainly understandable that when his two youngest boys reached college age that W.T. Vaughn would entrust their higher education to his former Cordell Christian colleague and friend J.N. Armstrong and the Harding College faculty. Harding College remained in Morrilton until 1938 when the school acquired the old Galloway College property in

The former Galloway College property was acquired by Harding College in 1938.

Searcy, Arkansas, allowing the college to double its capacity and continue its physical growth as well as its influence throughout the United States and foreign countries. It soon became a respected institution of higher education and spiritual development which it continues to enjoy today.

A HARDING BASKETBALL STAR IS BORN

On November 27, 1934, brothers Paul and Raymond Vaughn

reported for the first day of varsity basketball practice, along with four returning lettermen and 16 other freshmen hoop hopefuls. It was the largest group of hardcourt candidates in years and there was some thought given to the possibility of having to cut the squad due to limited equipment and practice facilities.

The underclassmen years of being a freshman and sophomore are often spent finding one's strengths and weaknesses while jockeying for position and notice amongst the larger college classes. Such was the case for the Vaughn boys. Following their freshman year at Harding, Paul, already a year older than Raymond, had exited the college life in search of a career in the United States

Sophomore photo of Raymond Vaughn from the Harding *Petit Jean* Yearbook.

Navy. Raymond remained in Arkansas, working during his summer vacations at a local grain mill and constructing homes, an experience that would serve him well in later life as he often supplemented his teaching and coaching income with real estate development and construction projects. During his sophomore year Raymond continued his educational pursuits and began to distinguish himself through his athletic, leadership, and social skills.

It was during his junior year, as an upperclassman in 1936-1937, that Vaughn hit his stride as a "big" man on campus in more than one way. Not only was he chosen to be the captain of the basketball team and president of the lettermen's club, known as the "H" Club, but, being a bit undersized as a basketball forward at 5'11" tall, his point production on the team gave him the status of a giant through his play on the court. It was about that time, as well, that his fellow students noticed the uncharacteristically large size of his feet, which were size 12, and affectionately gave him the nickname "Foots". The name stuck with him through the remainder of his life.

Vaughn's reputation on the court was certainly enhanced during his final years at Harding through the publication of the school newspaper,

| COLEMAN | SHANNON | VAUGHN | BARTON |
| Forward | Guard | Forward | Guard |

Harding College Bison starting guards and forwards for the 1936-1937 season.

The Bison. The February 2, 1937 edition contains the following account of the trouncing administered to the Little Rock Junior College team by the Harding varsity, known as "The Herd:"

BISONS ANNEX 57 TO 21 WIN OVER TROJANS HERD EASILY TAKES FIFTH VICTORY OF CURRENT SEASON

Vaughn Leads Team

With Captain "Foots" Vaughn leading the way with 22 points, the Herd annexed its third straight victory and it's fifth of the season by swamping Little Rock Junior College 57 to 21 at Little Rock Tuesday night.

The Bison jumped into an early lead and were never threatened by the inexperienced junior collegians although they played a fast game. Although they missed as many shots as they made, the Bison were in possession of the ball most of the time and had piled up a 33 to 8 lead at the half way mark.

The boy's basketball team in the Harding College Gymnasium.

  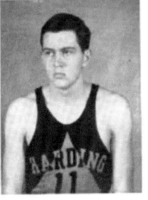

RAYMOND VAUGHN
Forward
Captain

JOE LEWIS LESLIE
Guard

JOSEPH E. PRYOR
Center
Alternate-Captain

Raymond "Foots" Vaughn leads the Harding Bison Basketball Team in scoring and as the team captain his junior year.

Vaughn was largely responsible for this lead by his 18 points, scored in the initial period.

With 9 field goals and 4 free tosses to his credit, Vaughn led the entire field in scoring with a total of 22 points, which brought his average to 15.4 points for the seven games he has played. In all, he has accounted for 108 of the Bison's total points. Pryor, center, and Watts, forward, hit the bucket for 12 points each to tie for second place honors.

In his sports column, "Sportorically Speaking", in the same edition quoted above, Gene Pace made the following observation: "Captain 'Foots' Vaughn is going right on up with his average score in games played this season. In fact, he should be among the top scorers in the state if the press of the state will give him half of a chance—which they haven't done yet. His average through Wednesday night was 15.4 points a game. He has accounted for 108 points in seven contests. And, oddly enough, he is far

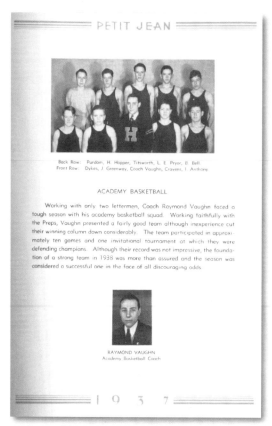

ACADEMY BASKETBALL

Working with only two lettermen, Coach Raymond Vaughn faced a tough season with his academy basketball squad. Working faithfully with the Preps, Vaughn presented a fairly good team although inexperience cut their winning column down considerably. The team participated in approximately ten games and one invitational tournament at which they were defending champions. Although their record was not impressive, the foundation of a strong team in 1938 was more than assured and the season was considered a successful one in the face of all discouraging odds.

RAYMOND VAUGHN
Academy Basketball Coach

1937

Early coaching experience for Coach Raymond Vaughn included the Harding Academy High School squad of 1937.

ahead of the rest of the squad in that department."

By the time he finished at Harding, Coach Vaughn had already acquired a modicum amount of experience at coaching basketball. It was common for one of the varsity team members to also serve as the coach for the Harding Academy High School squad. As the captain of Harding's varsity team it would have been an expectation that Coach Vaughn would likewise be the academy coach his junior year. The 1937 *Petit Jean* Yearbook devoted an entire page to that year's academy team and its coach.

VAUGHN'S SENIOR YEAR IS MARRED BY INJURY

As Raymond Vaughn prepared for what would possibly be his crowning college achievement, his senior basketball season as team captain and high point production star of the Harding Bison "Herd", he is stricken

Raymond Vaughn had to sit out his senior basketball season because of a knee injury. However, he continued to serve as captain of the team.

with a knee injury that not only requires his sitting out that season of play, while continuing his duties as team captain, but his withdrawal from active participation in classes for the semester. It is unclear exactly what caused the issue with his knee; however, during his naval career he resorted to knee surgery before continuing his tour of duty in the South Pacific. As a result of this condition, Vaughn did not graduate with his class in the summer of 1938 and instead finished his degree the following fall, graduating from Harding College in early 1939.

When he completed his career at Harding College in 1939, Vaughn had accumulated an impressive list of accomplishments

Raymond Vaughn graduated from Harding University in 1939 with a bachelor's degree in History.

in addition to his bachelor's degree in History. He served as vice president of his Social Service Club, was a two-year captain of the varsity basketball team, two-year president of the Letterman's "H" Club; president of the Oklahoma Club, and named "Boy Favorite" his senior year.

INDUCTION INTO THE HARDING UNIVERSITY ATHLETIC HALL OF FAME

In 1992, twelve years after his untimely death and 53 years after his graduation, his widow, Sue Vaughn, was notified that Coach Raymond Vaughn would be posthumously inducted into the Harding University Athletic Hall of Fame in honor of his outstanding basketball career while on campus and his stellar coaching career thereafter. In the Harding University gymnasium, his place of honor is among the elite athletes that have competed throughout the years in the green and gold of Harding University. Although this recognition honors his contributions during the early part of his athletic and educational career, he was to be inducted into no less than five more halls of fame before his storybook career is tragically ended by brain cancer at the age of 63.

At this point, Coach Vaughn is ready to make his mark on society by entering the educational field and continuing the coaching career that he so dearly loved. He never returned to the wheat fields of western Oklahoma, although his family members still own that quarter-section of farm land that he grew up on southwest of Cordell. It was a career that was short lived, at least for that moment. No one could have predicted

Coach Raymond Vaughn was posthumously inducted into the Harding Athletic Hall of Fame in 1992.

how that career would be interrupted, almost before it got started, when

Japan bombed Pearl Harbor and brought World War II to our shores.

United States Naval Officer Raymond L. Vaughn in his dress whites.

CHAPTER THREE

A Quick Start to a Long & Successful Coaching Career

Upon graduation from Harding University in 1939, Vaughn was employed by the Pleasant Plains School District in Pleasant Plains, Arkansas as a physical education director and high school basketball coach. He produced a District Championship team the following year.

During the summer of 1940, when school was out, the young coach served as Community Welfare Director before returning to his basketball coaching duties in the fall. Once again he led his teams to championships in both the A and B divisions.

In September of 1941, having garnered the attention of many in the coaching field, Vaughn was offered the position of director of intramurals at the University of Oklahoma (OU) in Norman. He accepted and was given the responsibility of overseeing, scheduling, and even officiating intramural sporting events for 5,000 male students. While at OU, Vaughn began work on his master's degree in Physical Education.

INTERRUPTED BY A DECLARATION OF WAR

On January 28, 1942, a little over a month and a half following the Japanese attack on Pearl Harbor, Coach Ray Vaughn enlisted in the United States Navy. While waiting on his acceptance into the Navy,

The United States Naval enlistment photo of Raymond Vaughn.

Chief Petty Officer Raymond L. Vaughn.

Vaughn returns to Searcy, Arkansas where he fills in as the superintendent of nearby West Point Public Schools. While there he oversees one Grade A high school and three Grade B junior high and elementary schools. As superintendent he was directly responsible to the State Board of Education of Arkansas.

On April 6, 1942, Vaughn takes his oath of office and begins a distinguished naval career as a chief petty officer in the United States Navy.

Vaughn's first naval assignment was for "physical instruction" at Norfolk, Virginia where he spent the first eight weeks of his military career. He was then assigned to the U.S. Naval Training Center in Great Lakes, Illinois where he

The U.S. Naval Training Center in Great Lakes, Illinois.

continued his training and subsequently made application for permanent appointment as an Ensign D-V (S) in the United States Naval Reserve.

Vaughn's military record contains the following response from his commanding officer to the Chief of Naval Personnel:

> The Officer Procurement Section of the Selection Office has interviewed the subject man and as a result of such interview, considers him to be qualified for appointment as Ensign, D-V (S), (General Sea Duty Officer), U.S. Naval Reserve. Subject man has an excellent personality...presents a good appearance and has a military bearing. He is poised, confident, well-mannered, brisk and alert. He is otherwise considered to be excellent officer material.

On December 18, 1943 Chief Petty Officer Raymond Vaughn received his appointment to the United States Naval Reserve with the rank of Ensign, D-V (S). Ensign Vaughn is then ordered to report to the commanding officer at the Naval Training School located at the University

Graduation from the Naval Training School at the University of Arizona in Tucson. Chief Petty Officer Raymond Vaughn is located on the left, third step.

of Arizona in Tucson for temporary active duty.

Following two weeks of what was termed "indoctrination" training at the University of Arizona, Vaughn was once again on the move. From there Vaughn receives "advanced" training at Fort Schuyler in The Bronx, New York and on June 5, 1944 is ordered to proceed to Melville, Rhode Island where he is to report to the commanding officer, Motor Torpedo Boat Squadrons Training Center, Portsmouth, for "temporary duty under instruction, pending further assignment to duty afloat."

Having completed Motor Torpedo Boat training, Vaughn is

reassigned on October 17, 1944 to the Office of the Commandant of the Twelfth Naval District and sent to San Francisco, California for assignment to duty.

On February 9, 1945, Ensign Vaughn is sent into the battle zone and assigned to PT Boat Base 21, known as "Stinker" in U.S. Navy Code, at Mios Woendi, an atoll in the

Ensign Raymond Vaughn is assigned to PT Boat Base 21 in the Schouten Islands, southeast of Biak, Indonesia.

Schouten Islands, southeast of Biak, Indonesia. "Stinker" was one of the Navy's forward bases during World War II. Upon arrival, Ensign Vaughn is attached to Motor Torpedo Boat Squadron 23 where his duties aboard PT284 include boat executive officer and navigation officer.

On the 1st day of April, 1945, Ensign Vaughn is promoted to Lieutenant (jg). After a brief stay on the USS *Cyrene* and at a naval hospital in San Francisco, where he had successful surgery on his right knee, Vaughn returned to Squadron 23 and resumed his duties as the third officer on PT286.

MOTOR TORPEDO (PT) BOATS

Patrol Torpedo "PT" Boats were used extensively during World War II in the Pacific. Their small size, speed, maneuverability, and heavy armament made them particularly adept at stalking and attacking enemy watercraft in coastal waters.

Lieutenant (jg) Vaughn serves on both PT Boats 284 as executive and navigation officer and on 286 as third officer.

PT Boats could house a crew of three officers and twelve sailors. Each were equipped with four torpedo tubes and two deck mounted .50 caliber machine guns. In addition, some carried a 20mm cannon as well. They were powered by three Packard V-12 aircraft engines that could generate a top speed of around 45 miles per hour.

The boats were hated by the Japanese who referred to them as "devil boats". Their success and intrigue was significantly enhanced following the war when the public learned that future President of the United States, John F. Kennedy, had once captained PT109.

THE END NEARS FOR JAPAN

On August 6, 1945 the United States dropped an atomic bomb on

Hiroshima, Japan. Three days later, on August 9th, a second atomic bomb is released over Nagasaki. Six days later, on August 15, 1945, Japanese Emperor Hirohito announces Japan's surrender.

TAKING COMMAND

On August 31, 1945 Lieutenant (jg) Vaughn is made the Captain of PT243, a position he would hold through October by which time the war has officially ended and he is on his way home.

Little is known about Lieutenant Vaughn's time spent with Squadron 23 other than he participated in the invasion of Palawan, in the Philippines. The invasion resulted in the defeat of the Japanese Army and the establishment of an American air base on the island. As a result, Vaughn earns the Philippine Liberation Ribbon with Bronze Star. On the 2nd of September, 1945 Japan officially surrenders aboard the USS *Missouri*.

With the war over, the Navy begins the process of bringing sailors home. No longer needing the more than one thousand PT Boats produced during the conflict, many of the craft are given to other governments or, in

Lieutenant (jg) Vaughn is promoted to Captain of PT243 on August 31, 1945 shortly after

Captain Vaughn and his crew on PT243.

PT Boat Captain Raymond Vaughn, second from right, at "Stinker" base in the South China Sea.

the case of PT243, intentionally beached and burned. A few were sold as military surplus and remain in existence today as an honored memory of a war fought in close quarters in the waters of the Pacific.

The Philippine Liberation Ribbon with Bronze Star.

GOING HOME

On the first of November, 1945 Lieutenant (jg) Vaughn receives orders to "proceed immediately and report to the Commanding Officer, Receiving Station, Navy 3149, Tubabao, Philippine Islands for temporary duty awaiting assignment by the Chief of Naval Personnel."

While awaiting his transport back to the states, Vaughn spends most of that November in Tubabao. In his Officers

Following the war, PT243 is beached and burned along with many others.

Fitness Report of November 25th it is noted that "This officer has had considerable experience in organizing college athletic programs and in physical education. He would be an ideal recreation officer for a large activity."

Following a brief assignment in New Orleans, Louisiana, on January 12, 1946 Vaughn is ordered to report to the Commanding Officer of the U.S. Naval Personnel Separation Center for temporary additional duty in connection with welfare and recreation. Although eligible for release to inactive duty in February, Vaughn requests several active duty extensions which allow him to spend the rest of the winter, spring, and summer coaching young sailors in Norman, Oklahoma that are preparing for their return to civilian life. His first assignment is as an assistant welfare and recreation officer in charge of swimming.

Lieutenant (jg) Vaughn, standing right, returns to coaching softball following the war at a temporary Naval Base in Norman, Oklahoma.

Guthrie, Oklahoma, native Kenneth Mitchell was a 17-year-old naval recruit that fondly recalled his time with Lieutenant (jg) Vaughn on the base in Norman. He noted that there were at least three guys on base for every assignment. They were there awaiting their release from the service and there was not a lot to do. Mitchell's job was to unlock and lock the swimming pool every day. Others performed related duties such as lifeguarding and pool maintenance. There was so little to do that on occasion Mitchell would open the pool in Norman, take the train to his home in Guthrie, and return the same way that night in time to lock up.

On other occasions, Mitchell recalled playing on a softball team coached by Vaughn. "We fielded a full softball team with two subs. I was one of the subs. Back then, most of the small cities around Norman had softball teams, so Lieutenant Vaughn would drive the bus and we would leave the base most evenings and drive to Pauls Valley or Duncan or some other town and play softball. I remember one night the field where we played was right next to a pig farm. Most of the guys on the team, that weren't from Oklahoma, had never seen a pig before so they spent a lot of their time watching the pigs."

Mitchell recalls that there were some "pretty good ballplayers" on one of those teams. One in particular was Rudy Rufer who went on to play baseball for Dartmouth and OU, eventually signing with the Philadelphia Phillies. Rufer actually played a couple of seasons as a short stop for the New York Giants. In his last professional game in 1950, Rufer went 1 for 3 at the plate against Warren Spahn as his Giants beat the Boston Braves 5-1. Rufer died in 2010 at the age of 83.

In addition to softball, Lieutenant (jg) Vaughn also coached basketball, obviously drawing on his experiences as a player, team captain and coach while at Harding University.

While performing his "welfare and recreation" duties in Norman, Vaughn also took the necessary classes at the University of Oklahoma to complete his master's degree (MA) in Physical Education. On August 22, 1946, Vaughn is released to inactive duty after having served four years,

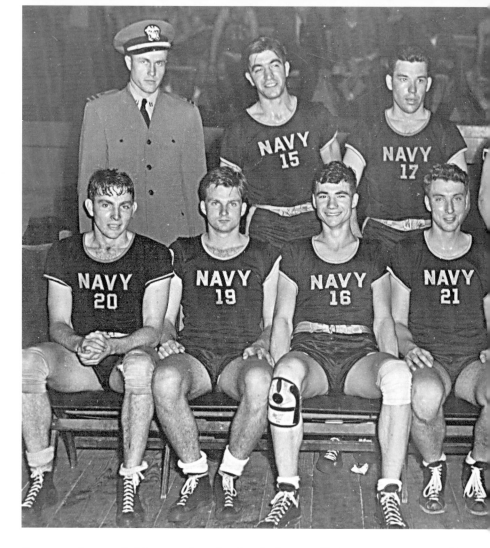

five months, and thirteen days in the defense of his country. One of his final fitness reports states, "This officer is well qualified for the work assigned him and takes the responsibility that goes with the job. He has experience at sea and as an enlisted man. He will do an excellent job at anything that his experience and education qualifies him to undertake. He has demonstrated leadership and is very capable and dependable. His

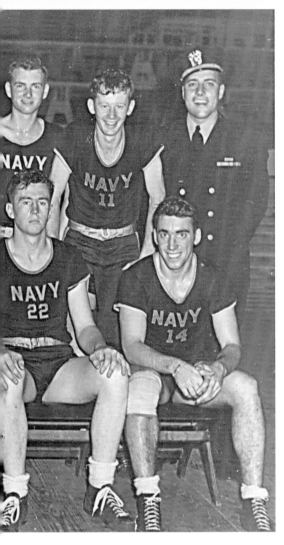

Coach Vaughn also coached his Naval basketball team to victory. Back Row, from left, R.C. Moore, S.A. Baptist, Dick Camp, Bill Gibbs, Dick Dart, and Raymond Vaughn. Front row, Harly Day, Bob Braly, Claude Overton, U.S. Grant, Gene Doherty, and Lew Rose.

conduct and military bearing are beyond reproach."

In his Notice of Separation from U.S. Naval Service, Vaughn is notified that he is entitled to wear the American Campaign Medal, Asiatic-Pacific Campaign Medal, Philippine Liberation Campaign Ribbon (one star), and the Victory Medal.

On October 14, 1946 Vaughn requests a transfer to the Organized

Naval Reserve. This request is granted three weeks later and he is assigned to Organized Reserve Division 8-44 where he is given the assignment of education and training officer. The following summer, Vaughn reports to the USS *Haynsworth* for a training cruise. He is assigned to the gunnery department. He scored high marks on his performance and his training evaluation states that "He showed great interest and enthusiasm for all training conducted. With more training Lieutenant (jg) Vaughn would become a very good naval officer."

On the 1st day of January 1949, Vaughn is promoted to the rank of lieutenant in the U.S. Naval Reserve, a position he will hold for the next five years until he is honorably discharged on the 15th day of July, 1954 ending his military service.

A SON'S THANKS *by Raymond L. Vaughn, Jr.*

Like many who have served in the military, Raymond L. Vaughn did not talk much, if at all, about his service or assignments in the Navy. Therefore, other than a few photographs of him in his uniform, especially those at his wedding, there was little knowledge our family had about his experiences in World War II. As a result, I would like to extend our personal debt of gratitude and sincere appreciation to the United States Government for not only keeping dad's military records intact but also for making them available to family members like ourselves for only a nominal charge for duplication. If you would like to have copies of your veteran's military history there are a number of sites on the internet that can answer your questions as to how to obtain them. Virtually none of what is contained in this chapter could have been included in this book without such records.

It was a pleasure to discover Dad's exploits and travels during his active duty years with the Navy. His service makes us proud to think of a western Oklahoma farm boy taking leadership of a crew and high performance battle weapon, like a PT boat, and succeeding in the defeat of an enemy that sought the destruction of our country and way of life.

Coach Ray Vaughn with members of a Capitol Hill High School relay team.

CHAPTER FOUR

A Dream Job at Capitol Hill High School

Following his service in the Navy, Lieutenant Raymond Vaughn resumed civilian life in Oklahoma City and started courting a young lady to whom he had been introduced by family friends. Ava Miles Hisel, who had been nicknamed "Sue" by an uncle, was a teacher of drama and speech in the Putnam City School District. On the 30th day of August, 1946 the two were married and settled in a modest home at 409 S.W. 35th Street on the northwest corner of S. W. 35th Street and S. Walker Avenue, just one block north of Capitol Hill High School.

In the fall of that year, Coach Vaughn began his new job as the head track coach, assistant football and basketball coach, and physical education teacher at Capitol Hill High School. At the time Capitol Hill was the only high school south of the Canadian River, known today as the "Oklahoma River". Because of its size, range of subjects, and sports teams, the "Redskins" were considered one of

Raymond Vaughn married Ava Miles "Sue" Hisel on August 30, 1946 in southwest Oklahoma City.

Mr. Raymond L. Vaughn
Subject: Football, Track
Sponsorship: Boys' O Club,
, Football, Sophomore Class

Raymond Vaughn's faculty photo
from the Capitol Hill High School
yearbook. *Courtesy the Capitol Hill
High School* Chieftain.

the dominant schools in the Oklahoma City School District; however, that had not always been the case.

A VERY HUMBLE BEGINNING

In 1926 the Oklahoma City School District had 28,089 school-aged children to educate. The largest school in the system was Lee Elementary, at S.W. 29th Street and S. Walker Avenue, with an enrollment of 2,154. Five years earlier, Capitol Hill Junior High had opened with a student population of 800 and had doubled in size by 1926, suggesting that a much larger high school would soon be needed. The school board quickly responded with a 16-room addition to the existing junior high facility which was renamed the Capitol Hill Junior-Senior High School.

In 1929 the $500,000.00 Capitol Hill High School campus opened on a twenty-acre site on the southwest corner of S.W. 36th Street and S. Walker Avenue in south Oklahoma City. Enrollment that year reached its zenith with an unprecedented 2,000 students utilizing all 50 classrooms in the main building, four outlying structures, and

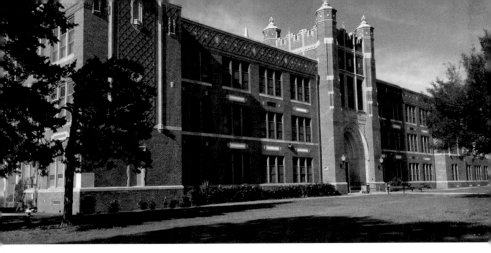
Capitol Hill High School opened in 1929 to a record enrollment of 2,000.

three classrooms in the nearby Lee Elementary School. Administrators were offering "424 different credit courses including college preparatory and general education classes, vocational and technical training and work in merchandising, selling and the trades." Operating an educational facility of such mammoth proportions was no easy task. The daily curriculum and facilities required "77 teachers, three administrators, six clerks, two counselors, a fulltime nurse and some 18 custodians."

"MILLION DOLLAR" FIELD HOUSE

Already known for its academic and athletic achievements, Capitol Hill High School administrators gained national attention when they proposed a "first of its kind" round-roofed field house as an addition to their campus. The facility, sometimes referred to as the "coffee pot" due to its circular design, would house all indoor sporting activities as well as musical events.

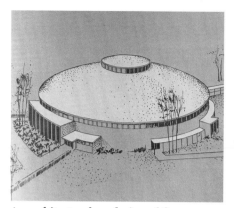

An architectural rendering of the new Capitol Hill High School Field House and Gymnasium. *Courtesy the Capitol Hill High School* Chieftain.

The Capitol Hill High School Field House under construction in 1954. *Courtesy the Capitol Hill High School* Chieftain.

The central basketball court, featured on the ground floor of the facility, hosted all of Capitol Hill's home basketball games and wrestling matches. Floor and balcony seating offered over 5,000 unobstructed spectator seats to any event. The Oklahoma City Board of Education approved construction of the field house on May 11, 1954 with an estimated cost of $1,000,000.00. Thirteen construction companies submitted bids on the project with a winning low bid of $790,000.00. Raymond Vaughn, in his role then as athletic director, played a significant role in overseeing the design and construction of the groundbreaking sporting venue.

Oklahoma City University (OCU) was the first team to play in the building as they abandoned their home court at the Oklahoma City Municipal Auditorium in favor of the new Capitol Hill showcase. The December 1, 1955 game was a success in all respects as OCU bested their opponent, Emporia State, and won the hearts of Capitol Hill residents in

The completed Capitol Hill High School Sports Arena.

the first college sporting event to be held south of the river in Oklahoma City. The *Capitol Hill Beacon* proudly pronounced that "the local field house is still one of the best in the state for basketball contests. And it can claim the distinction of setting the trend toward 'basketball shaped' field houses."

The Capitol Hill High School Field House bore the mascot name "Redskins" for 61 years.

Following protests of the use of the name "Redskins", in May of 2015, the Oklahoma City School Board voted to suspend the use of the name and the school's student body voted to change the schools 86-year-old mascot to the "Red Wolves". The name change was not without opposition from the alumni, including American Indians, which were proud of their accomplishments as "Redskins".

Ray Thompson graduated from Capitol Hill High School in 1951, during the heyday of Capitol Hill High School track and field under Coach Ray Vaughn. He went on to serve on the USS *Kula Gulf* during World War II before earning his degree in Business Education and a masters in Guidance and Counseling from Central State University.

Former Capitol Hill High School graduate and principal Ray Thompson. *Courtesy of Ray Thompson.*

Ray has taught or served in an administration role for a number of Oklahoma City Public Schools for almost thirty years, including a stint as principal of Capitol Hill High School from 1973 to 1978. He has been the Commissioner of High School Football Officials and has served on the Oklahoma City Game and Fish Commission, the Parks Commission, and the Oklahoma City Judicial Review Committee. His service includes serving as a board member of the new downtown Oklahoma City John Rex Charter Elementary School and he has been inducted into the Oklahoma Secondary Schools Football Officials Hall of Fame and the Capitol Hill High School Athletic and Activites Association Hall of Fame.

Of his experience at Capitol Hill, Thompson writes, "When asked to reflect on my cherished days as a student at our wonderful Capitol Hill High School from 1948 to 1951, I was very happy to do so. I considered it an honor and a privilege to serve as the student manager of our 1949 undefeated state championship football team coached by John Miskovsky,

C.B. Speegle, and Ray Vaughn, who also coached our state championship track team during the 1950 and 1951 seasons. The track team set state records in the 880- and one-mile relay, as well as the individual 440-yard dash run by J.W. Mashburn. I was also proud to be the sports editor of the school yearbook and newspaper.

"As I look back on those days I recognize what outstanding teachers and role models we were blessed to have on our faculty. After serving as a teacher, coach, counselor, and assistant principal in seven secondary Oklahoma City Schools, I had the honor of becoming the principal, for five years, of our old high school. I will always have wonderful memories of being a Capitol Hill Redskin."

AN OUTSTANDING TEAM OF COACHES

From its first fielding of a football team in 1923, Capitol Hill High School quickly amassed impressive statistics in virtually all sports. The availability of amazing athletic talent, coupled with the recruitment of an outstanding team of coaches, very soon made Capitol Hill High School a sports power to be reckoned with.

Early-day Capitol Hill High School football coach Jim Lookabaugh went on to coach Oklahoma A & M to its only unbeaten-untied football season in 1945. *Courtesy Oklahoma Hall of Fame.*

One of the first "big name" coaches at Capitol Hill was E. M. "Jim" Lookabaugh. He headed the coaching staff from 1930 through 1938 before ultimately coaching at Oklahoma A&M College, known today as Oklahoma State University (OSU). Lookabaugh's

Sue and Ray Vaughn at a Capitol Hill High School banquet.

high school football coaching career is still remembered for two of his seasons. In 1930, his first year as head coach, his team was shut out with an 0-8-2 record only to be followed in 1933 with a perfect 12-0 record, including the state championship.

One contributing factor to the coaching successes at Capitol Hill High School was the collegiality and cooperation among the coaching staff. For example, while Coach Vaughn headed up the track team and ultimately served as athletic director, he also served as an assistant coach on the football team. Other coaches did the same, leading to a "team" attitude not only among the athletes but among the coaches as well.

Dick Soergel attended Capitol Hill High School from 1953 through 1956. He was the school's last three-sport letterman playing football for C.B. Speegle, basketball for John Smith, and baseball for John Pryor. He says he did not run track because there was no "turtle team."

Dick Soergel was a three-sport letterman at Capitol Hill High School—lettering in football, basketball, and baseball. *Courtesy Dick Soergel.*

After graduating from Capitol Hill High School he went on to letter in three sports at Oklahoma State University and even signed to play professional football with the Boston Patriots during the first year of the American Football League. After being cut from the squad, he returned to Stillwater and became the business manager for the OSU Athletic Department where he worked for 16 years before going into banking and trust asset

Administrator and businessman Dick Soergel. *Courtesy Dick Soergel.*

management. He believes he knows the key to what he calls Capitol Hill's "athletic dominance" of high school sports during those years.

Soergel explained, "We had outstanding coaches. It wasn't just one, it was all of them. C.B. Speegle was the head football coach, John Smith coached basketball, and John Pryor was the baseball coach. Ray Vaughn was the track coach and athletic director and it was Coach Vaughn as the AD that held all that together. He kept those coaches together. To me he was a man of real character. He was a discipline person and he had his routines for you and he didn't mess around. You had to fall in line and do it the way he wanted you to do it. But he was so good at keeping people together and keeping those coaches together. He was the guy that also kept a handle on the finances because he was such a man of character and discipline. He was also a Christian. His values were something that he expressed through his actions. I really appreciated Coach Vaughn. I liked all the coaches, but he was such a fine gentleman. I respected him so much."

It was a common practice at the time for the coaches to participate with the other faculty members in school events such as banquets and even theatrical productions. The coaches even found time to

A Capitol Hill High School coaches' basketball team, back row, from left, C.B. Speegle, Don Van-pool, Ladarrell Scott, and John Miskovsky. Front Row, Cheesy Littlefield, Ray Vaughn, unknown, unknown, John Smith, and E.G. Stewart.

compete together as is evidenced by this undated team photo of the faculty basketball team.

In addition to his other duties, one of the first assignments to face the young coach Vaughn was to build a competitive track program and recruit students to fill the variety of events from sprinters to distance runners on the track and from the weight events to the jumpers in the field events. The major sports of football, basketball, baseball and wrestling were well established with a litany of participants ready to compete each year. Track, however, was a different story. This was a relatively new program which had to be built from the ground up.

Fortunately, with his pick from all students on the south side of Oklahoma City, many of whom wanted to compete but were not already "plugged in" to one of the major sports, Vaughn had the opportunity, as the physical education teacher in mandatory physical education classes to "discover" new athletes to fill the positions on his track team.

CHASING JACK RABBITS

Don Ladd came to Capitol Hill High School from a farm west of Oklahoma City. He grew up playing sandlot softball and football but spent most of his time chasing jack rabbits and riding his bicycle up and down the gravel roads. He really didn't know much about the sport of track.

Don Ladd, a Capitol Hill High School student athlete coached by Raymond Vaughn. *Courtesy Don Ladd.*

"Coach Vaughn was my gym teacher as well as the track coach. One day, he took the entire gym class out to the track and announced that we were to all run a mile, four laps around the track. Coach was timing us and so I just took off like I was chasing another jack rabbit, not fast, but steady. I have no idea what my time was that day but I finished way ahead of everyone because a lot of them walked," Ladd remembered.

He continued, "He came up to me the next day in gym class and asked if I would like to join the track team. At 5' 7" and 130 pounds, I was not a candidate for football or basketball so I thought, why not? As it turned out, I was the individual state cross country champion in 1951 and earned a track scholarship at OU from another great track coach—John Jacobs.

I had made no plans to go on to college from high school. I just wanted to graduate and find a job somewhere. Had Coach Vaughn not taken that gym class out to the track I would never have known that I had a talent that would provide a college education. He not only encouraged me to join the team, but he insisted that I train hard to make the best of my talents. Coach Vaughn was not only a wonderful coach, but he was also a thoughtful and kind person who probably affected my life as much as anyone."

Don Ladd graduated from the University of Oklahoma and has enjoyed successful careers in the savings and loan and real estate fields in the metropolitan Oklahoma City area.

Jim "Whitey" White was the Vaughn family paper boy and lived just a block north of Coach Vaughn. His first acquaintance with Coach Vaughn came through the recreational program administered by the coach for *The Daily Oklahoman* and their south side paper carriers.

During the winter months Coach Vaughn oversaw a south side basketball league in the Capitol Hill gymnasium, followed by a summer softball league held at Wheeler Park in south Oklahoma City. White recalls, "He was known for his skill in training young men to become outstanding track and field athletes, but probably more importantly as a Christian man of genuine integrity. Foul language was not a part of his vocabulary and high standards of character were his expectation of himself and of others."

MASTER OF MOTIVATION

White wanted to participate in competitive athletics; however, his newspaper delivery business had kept him from trying out for the highly popular football, basketball, and baseball teams that had numerous players who had waited years for a chance at a starting position. So, as Whitey tells it "on a fateful day, I showed up for a fall cross-country workout. It was a Monday and I happened to arrive on the very day that they were having a two-mile time trial.

"Coach Vaughn had laid out a one-mile course beginning from the south side of the school property over to Walker, then down Walker to S.W. 44th Street, then west on 44th to Western, then back north along Western and back toward Walker to the starting point. Twice around that course was two miles. I had not had any preparation for the rigor of that event or that day. When I finished, I was in the most excruciating pain that I had ever felt. What motivated me to finish was a speech that Coach Vaughn gave just before we started.

Jim "Whitey" White delivered papers to the Vaughn household and took advantage of the recreational program offered through *The Daily Oklahoman. Courtesy Jim White.*

"Coach Vaughn said, 'If you begin this run today, you will finish it. You may have to walk part of it, you may have to slow down for a while. But, if you begin this run, I expect you to finish it. I will be at the finish. I will wait on you. But again, I remind you that I expect you to finish however late it may be. I believe you can finish and I will see you in a while.'

Jim "Whitey" White was a member of the Capitol Hill High School track team. *Courtesy the Capitol Hill High School* Chieftain.

"I almost blacked out, but I was glad that I tried. It was a time of my life when I began to see in myself more than I had imagined before. A large part of that was the speech given on that hot September day in 1954 when Ray Vaughn told us that he believed in us."

A QUIET DISCIPLINARIAN

Whitey remembered that "on one of our road trips to Fort Worth, Texas our team did not do as well as we knew we could. Both of our 440- and 880-sprint relay teams were disqualified due to simple mental errors. One runner actually left the baton lying next to the starting blocks when the gun sounded. When we began the trip home, we stopped about half way for a rest stop. One of Coach Vaughn's training rules was that we should never drink soda pop. When we got back on the bus two of our sprinters returned with sodas. Vaughn said, 'Go put your pop back young men. Don't bring it on the bus.' They chose to defy him.

"Coach said nothing until we had arrived back in the parking lot at the school where he took his place in the front of the bus to address the team. He said, 'Fellows, we did not do as well as I expected in Fort Worth and I know we can do better. I will see you Monday for workout. However, the two of you who brought your sodas on the bus are off the team. Take your bags to the locker room and leave them there. Do not return. I am sorry, but you are finished.'

"It was a sobering lesson in discipline, but an important one. Further, by the time the major meets began in Oklahoma our team had three sprinters who broke 10 flat for the hundred-yard dash. We were not diminished by the loss of those two."

"I COULDN'T WALK AND CHEW GUM AT THE SAME TIME"

At 6' 9" tall, Hub Reed played seven seasons in the National Basketball Association as a 1958 second round pick by the St. Louis Hawks. He later played with the Cincinnati Royals, Los Angeles Lakers, and finally with the Detroit Pistons, retiring with a career scoring mark of 2,618 points. Before his success in the NBA however, Hub played at Oklahoma City University under the tutelage of its famous coach Abe Lemons.

What prepared Hub for his successful career in basketball; however, was the time he spent at Capitol Hill High School with Coach Ray Vaughn. Reed, in *The Daily Oklahoman* article by sportswriter Berry Tramel featuring his life story, states "I was the tallest kid in school by far. I think we had 3,400 kids. Ray Vaughn was our athletic director. We had some athletes like J.W. Mashburn. Mr. Vaughn got me in his office and said, 'let me show you something.' He had a film of the Olympics in

times I've used Coach Vaughn as an example in one of my Bible lessons."

HIGH SCHOOL QUARTERBACK AND BABYSITTER

Dr. J. Don Harris graduated from Capitol Hill High School in 1955 and went on to graduate from the University of Central Oklahoma and the University of Missouri School of Dentistry, where he later served as an adjunct professor, and as chief of the dental staff at Saint Anthony's Hospital. He is the recipient of a number of community service awards and leadership positions. Dr. Harris has dedicated his practice to the preventative, restorative, and cosmetic dental work for all citizens, especially those with developmental and congenital disabilities and elderly Oklahomans who are in dire need of free comprehensive dental care due to the lack of financial resources.

When Coach and Mrs. Vaughn had plans for the evening, Coach Vaughn often asked J. Don to babysit their baby boy, Ray, Jr. Apparently he did a good job as Ray, Jr. successfully made it to adulthood.

"Coach Vaughn taught me more about being a man with character than anyone else ever did. He had eyes that could communicate what he was thinking and remove any doubt in your mind that he was right. I was around his family often and knew he was a good family man because many times he treated me and the other athletes like family," Harris remembered.

"I was the captain of the football team and played quarterback. Coach Vaughn was an assistant coach on the Capitol Hill High School varsity football team, but also was head coach of the 'B' squad. One week, Coach Vaughn asked me to dress out with the B team for an out-of-town game. I agreed. But when I got to the field I didn't have my football jersey. For some reason I hadn't put it in my game bag.

Former Capitol Hill High School football captain and quarterback Dr. J. Don Harris. *Courtesy J. Don Harris.*

"When it was time to warm up the team, Coach Vaughn told me to go out and lead the team in our pre-game calisthenics even though all I had to wear was the shirt I had worn to school that day which happened to be a red and black checked dress shirt. I did what the coach said, feeling very conspicuous and embarrassed in my dress shirt and remaining football uniform.

"When it was time to start the game the referee reminded the coach that I couldn't play without a football jersey, at which time Coach Vaughn produced an extra jersey for me to wear

Capitol Hill High School's quarterback J. Don Harris as he appeared in the school's yearbook. *Courtesy J. Don Harris.*

and the game got underway. Although it was an embarrassing moment, I know that Coach Vaughn was teaching me a responsibility lesson which, of course, worked. I never again forgot a piece of my football equipment or uniform. No one made more of an impression on me when I was growing up than Coach Vaughn."

THE GODFATHER OF TRACK

"The Godfather of Track," that is how Frank Taylor describes his former track coach at Capitol Hill. It is every bit a compliment in the way he says it. Frank was one of those guys that could have gone either way at that point in life. His father was not in the home at the time. He did not have a coat to keep him warm on his short walk to school or spending money in his pocket. What he had was God given. He had a friend in Coach Vaughn and he had an amazing amount of speed. He also, quite conveniently, lived between Coach Vaughn's house and the high school.

Taylor recalls, "Every morning Coach Vaughn would walk by my house on his way to school. He would stop and tap on my bedroom window to make sure I was up and getting ready for class. He wouldn't stop. He would just smile and wave and keep going."

Taylor remembers, "Coach Vaughn was a big influence on me. He was such an inspiration. He always had that big smile. I remember

Frank Taylor in the starting position for the Capitol Hill High School track team. *Courtesy Oklahoma Publishing Company.*

Coach Ray Vaughn. *Courtesy Capitol Hill High School Chieftain.*

it just like it was yesterday. People don't realize what an impression someone can make on a child and not even know it, but, Coach Vaughn knew it and that is why he always spoke to me. He was such a great person."

Taylor's goal had been to play baseball at Capitol Hill, and he did excel because of his speed. "I could lay down a bunt and beat the throw to first base" he said. "But, I really enjoyed running track and finally decided to concentrate on that." That decision certainly proved to be profitable for Taylor. His relay team, on which he ran the sprint position, set a new Mid-State record in the half-mile relay with a 1:32.2— the fastest time recorded in the 30-year history of the meet.

Taylor also equaled the meet record in the 100-yard dash with a 9.9 clocking and established a new meet record in the 220-yard dash with a time of 21.3. With those performances, Capitol Hill edged out their crosstown rival, Northwest Classen, with 66½ and 64½ points respectively.

Frank Taylor was not only an outstanding athlete, he excelled in his scholastic studies as well, qualifying as one of Capitol Hill's valedictorians. During his brief two years at Capitol Hill, Taylor won 38 medals in track, half of which were gold, and set two Mid-State records earning an equal number of state titles. His track career was long from being over when he received his high school diploma.

In what proved to be a foreshadowing of Coach Vaughn's next life experience in Christian education, the Capitol Hill coach had achieved success in working with Abilene Christian College

The Capitol Hill High School half-mile relay team, from left, Frank Taylor, Jim Ferrill, Dennis Mercer, and Tommy Levine. *Courtesy Frank Taylor.*

(ACC) and obtaining a scholarship for former Capitol Hill High School distance runner Laddie Nethercutt. Nethercutt had actually lived with the Vaughn family during a portion of his high school career.

Frank Taylor's relay team at Abilene Christian College from left, world record holder in the 220-low hurdles Calvin Cooley, Dennis Richardson who tied the world record in the 100-yard dash, Frank Taylor, and 1960 Olympic Gold Medalist Earl Young. *Courtesy Frank Taylor.*

In 1958, Taylor became the next "Redskin" to wear the ACC "Wildcat" purple and achieved the same successes with Abilene as he had with Capitol Hill. Abilene Christian was an NCAA Division I school at the time. Therefore, the competition was the best to be had. His teammates included Olympic gold medalist Bobby

Morrow and Pan-American Champion Bill Woodhouse. As a freshman Taylor ran a 48.5 second quarter-mile, tying a school record held by former ACC and Olympic quarter-miler Earl Young. He also posted a 9.6 second 100 as well as a 21.2 second 220.

Three-gold Olympic medalist Bobby Morrow.

In 1961 Taylor's ACC relay team, while competing in the Texas Relays, earned a clean sweep, winning the 440-, 880-, mile, two-mile, and distance medley (a race consisting of a relay of varying distances including the quarter-mile, half-mile, three-quarter mile and one-mile). In 2000, the Abilene Christian track and field team was dubbed the Texas Sports Dynasty of the Century by *Texas Monthly* Magazine. In 2002, Frank Taylor was inducted into the Capitol Hill High School Athletic Activities Association Hall of Fame.

A CHANCE ENCOUNTER
THAT CHANGED A LIFE

John Doughty ran track for Coach Vaughn at Capitol Hill from 1951 through 1953 before spending the next five years in the Navy. When he returned to Oklahoma

Former Capitol Hill High School and Oklahoma Christian University runner John Doughty. *Courtesy John Doughty.*

John Doughty at Oklahoma Christian University. *Courtesy Oklahoma Christian Aerie.*

City in September of 1958 he dropped by Capitol Hill High School to pick up his high school transcript with the intent of enrolling at Central State University (CSU), now the University of Central Oklahoma, in Edmond.

As he was leaving the school, Coach Vaughn was driving in. The two stopped talk and catch up. Doughty recalls, "Coach Vaughn told me about a new school that was moving from Bartlesville to Edmond called Central Christian College. He was to be the athletic director, track coach, and basketball coach, all in one. He asked me, on the spot, if I would accept a scholarship to run track for him. I said 'yes', sight unseen. Five minutes either way, I would have enrolled at CSU.

"I wouldn't have met my wife to be, taught at Putnam City, fathered three fine children, and established lifelong friendships had it not been for that chance encounter. Coach Vaughn was one of those unforgettable people that I've had the privilege of knowing. He was my hero."

COMING FULL CIRCLE

After leaving Capitol Hill to start the athletic department at Oklahoma Christian, Coach Vaughn recruited a young man by the name of Tom Hibbitts as a quarter-miler. After he graduated from OC Vaughn brought him back twice as an assistant track coach. Then, he was instrumental in helping him land a coaching job at Capitol Hill High School. Hibbitts remembers Coach Vaughn this way, "Without his confidence in me, I would have never finished college. He was a great influence on me and hundreds of other college kids. I had a very successful track team at Capitol Hill, especially my mile relay team. The one question the coach

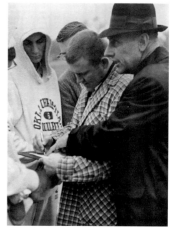

Coach Ray Vaughn and assistant coach Tom Hibbitts at an Oklahoma Christian track meet. *Courtesy Oklahoma Christian* Aerie.

had for me was, 'how did you get those boys to run the quarter-mile when I had hated to run it so much?' What a great man with a great legacy."

After leaving coaching, Hibbitts had a very successful career in the field of insurance. However, he continued his love of track by being the official starter for state high school and college meets for years, including Oklahoma Christian's Ray Vaughn Track Classic, an annual meet which honored the famed coach.

AN IMPRESSIVE RECORD

Ray Vaughn coached track and football, in addition to serving as athletic director, at Capitol Hill High School from

Tom Hibbitts, assistant track coach at Oklahoma Christian University. *Courtesy Tom Hibbitts.*

the fall of 1947 through the spring of 1958. During that time Vaughn's track teams were the Oklahoma City and Conference Champions in 1951, 1953, 1954, and 1955. Capitol Hill also won state track titles in 1950, 1951, and 1955. *The Daily Oklahoman* newspaper called Vaughn "the first track coach to break the dominance of the Tulsa schools."

LOOK, THEY HAVE LIGHTS DOWN THE SIDE OF THE ROAD

Coach Vaughn's wife, Sue Vaughn, being the younger of two daughters in her family, did not grow up with a natural appreciation of sports. Being a drama and speech teacher at heart she tended to lean more toward the performing arts and was quite a talent in her own right, having been an early performer in radio dramas on WKY Radio when its studios were located in the Skirvin Tower in downtown Oklahoma City.

She always made the effort to support her husband whenever there was a game, whether at home or away. When playing football games out of town, Coach Vaughn would always ride the team bus while Mrs. Vaughn was responsible for getting the rest of the family to the venue to cheer the team on. It was not necessary back then to know

A Vaughn family photo taken at their south Oklahoma City home.

the exact location of the opposing team's stadium as it was usually dark by the time the team and fans arrived and the lights of the stadium could easily be seen.

One night, Capitol Hill was playing at Shawnee. As Mrs. Vaughn and the family arrived in town it was clear from the lights where the stadium was located. Making their way towards the lights, they encountered a rather long, very straight road with ground lights down each side. About the time Mrs. Vaughn remarked as to the unusual placement of lights, Ray, Jr. realized they were on runway at the Shawnee Municipal Airport. Security was not what it is today and, thankfully, no one was landing or taking off at the time.

SOME TEACHERS LEAVE A LASTING IMPRESSION ON THEIR STUDENTS

Public school teachers that spend years on the job encounter literally thousands of students who remember their experiences, and their teachers, long after graduation. The Vaughn family was never surprised when someone would come up to them and relate the fact that Coach Vaughn was their teacher or coach at Capitol Hill. Most had very fond memories of their experiences; however, Ray, Jr. was somewhat unprepared and

Ray Vaughn, Jr. and his broadcasting mentor William H. "Bill" Payne.

amused as he observed first hand one of his father's encounters.

Ray Vaughn, Jr, recalled, "While in college at Oklahoma Christian University I decided to pursue a broadcasting career in radio and television. I was correctly advised to get some on-the-job training at a small radio station before attempting to break into the more sizeable Oklahoma City metro market and therefore, I had successfully approached my ultimate radio mentor William H. "Bill" Payne, owner of KWHP in Edmond about an internship.

"During the second semester of my junior year at OC, Bill proposed a marketing idea, which he dubbed a 'Wake-a-Thon', whereby I would attempt to break the world record for a live radio broadcast by a single individual which he said was 63 hours. I loved working for Bill and was gaining great experience; however, Bill was also quite a promoter and I had no idea whether there was actually a world record for such things or not, and really I didn't care. It sounded like fun so I accepted.

"Bill set out to acquire the necessary sponsorships for such a feat while I actually endured a physical exam by a local doctor, complete with photographs and a story which was submitted to the local *Edmond Evening Sun*, regarding whether I was physically fit enough to attempt such a grueling challenge, along with the proposed

The KWHP Radio Mobile Unit Ray Vaughn, Jr. used to set a new "Wake-a-Thon" record.

schedule, location, and of course, sponsors.

"KWHP had a 'mobile unit' which was essentially a large delivery van with windows in the back instead of doors, along with turntables and a microphone. It was comfortable for the disc jockey to sit in, along with a couple of others to sit behind the broadcaster. We parked the mobile unit on the east side of Broadway just south of 2nd Street in Edmond, erected the mobile transmitter and antenna back to the station, and were ready to alter world history. In broadcasting everything is about timing. So, we back timed from nine o'clock Saturday evening, which Bill figured would be a great time to gain maximum attention for a new world record and Sunday media exposure.

Ray Vaughn, Jr. and wife, Suzanne, in the KWHP Radio Mobile Unit on the first night of the "Wake-a-Thon".

"Sixty-three hours is a long time and actually required me to broadcast through almost three full days and two nights. I thought I would be fine during the daytime broadcasts; however, I was a bit concerned as to how I would fare during the overnight ones. My wonderful wife, Suzanne, wanted to sit with me through the first night [Thursday] and Dad, Coach Vaughn, volunteered for Friday night.

"Dad and I were enjoying each other's company that early Saturday morning about the time the only bar in Edmond shut down. The streets of downtown Edmond were empty with the exception of one car parked on the east side of Broadway in the first block of downtown north of 2nd Street. To the south of our studio we could see the lights of a single car driving slowly toward, and then past, our location at what might have been ten miles per hour. The very distinctive weave of the vehicle, even at that speed, indicated the probable intoxication of its driver.

"We watched as the vehicle went through the red light on the corner and plowed directly into the single parked car on the street. After what seemed like a reasonable time of observation with no movement detected, Dad said 'I guess I better go down there and see if anyone was hurt.' Dad walked the block and a half or so and returned some time later reporting that when he arrived on the scene the uninjured inebriant opened his car door and yelled, 'Coach Vaughn.'"

THE CAPITOL HILL ATHLETIC AND ACTIVITIES ASSOCIATION HALL OF FAME

In 2006, the former Capitol Hill High School athletic director, head track coach, as well as assistant football and assistant basketball coach, Ray Vaughn was posthumously inducted into the school's Hall of Fame. It is an honor shared with a number of his

Ray Vaughn, Jr. accepts a plaque acknowledging the induction of his father, Coach Raymond Vaughn, into the Capitol Hill Athletic and Activities Association Hall of Fame.

"Redskin" athletes that got their first encouragement in athletics from the rookie coach that they grew to love and respect. Many of them went on to perform well at the college and university level, some at the professional level, and even on the world stage of international competition including the Olympics. Ray, Jr. was privileged to receive the award and speak on his father's behalf at the annual banquet.

The Race

Attributed to Dr. D.H. "Dee" Groberg

Whenever I start to hang my head in front of failure's face,

my downward fall is broken by the memory of a race.

A children's race, young boys, young men; how I remember well,

excitement sure, but also fear, it wasn't hard to tell.

They all lined up so full of hope, each thought to win that race

or tie for first, or if not that, at least take second place.

Their parents watched from off the side, each cheering for their son,

and each boy hoped to show his folks that he would be the one.

The whistle blew and off they flew, like chariots of fire,

to win, to be the hero there, was each young boy's desire.

One boy in particular, whose dad was in the crowd,

was running in the lead and thought "My dad will be so proud."

But as he speeded down the field and crossed a shallow dip,

the little boy who thought he'd win, lost his step and slipped.

Trying hard to catch himself, his arms flew everyplace,

and midst the laughter of the crowd he fell flat on his face.

As he fell, his hope fell too; he couldn't win it now.

Humiliated, he just wished to disappear somehow.

But as he fell his dad stood up and showed his anxious face,

which to the boy so clearly said, "Get up and win that race!"

He quickly rose, no damage done, behind a bit that's all,

and ran with all his mind and might to make up for his fall.

So anxious to restore himself, to catch up and to win,

his mind went faster than his legs. He slipped and fell again.

He wished that he had quit before with only one disgrace.

"I'm hopeless as a runner now, I shouldn't try to race."

But through the laughing crowd he searched and found his father's face

with a steady look that said again, "Get up and win that race!"

So he jumped up to try again, ten yards behind the last.

"If I'm to gain those yards," he thought, "I've got to run real fast!"

Exceeding everything he had, he regained eight, then ten...

but trying hard to catch the lead, he slipped and fell again.

Defeat! He lay there silently. A tear dropped from his eye.

"There's no sense running anymore! Three strikes I'm out! Why try?

I've lost, so what's the use?" he thought. "I'll live with my disgrace."

But then he thought about his dad, who soon he'd have to face.

"Get up," an echo sounded low, "you haven't lost at all,

for all you have to do to win is rise each time you fall.

Get up!" the echo urged him on, "Get up and take your place!

   You were not meant for failure here! Get up and win that race!"

So, up he rose to run once more, refusing to forfeit,

   and he resolved that win or lose, at least he wouldn't quit.

So far behind the others now, the most he'd ever been,

   still he gave it all he had and ran like he could win.

Three times he'd fallen stumbling, three times he rose again.

   Too far behind to hope to win, he still ran to the end.

They cheered another boy who crossed the line and won first place,

   head high and proud and happy -- no falling, no disgrace.

But, when the fallen youngster crossed the line, in last place,

   the crowd gave him a greater cheer for finishing the race.

And even though he came in last with head bowed low, unproud,

   you would have thought he'd won the race, to listen to the crowd.

And to his dad he sadly said, "I didn't do so well."

   "To me, you won," his father said. "You rose each time you fell."

And now when things seem dark and bleak and difficult to face,

   the memory of that little boy helps me in my own race.

For all of life is like that race, with ups and downs and all.

   And all you have to do to win is rise each time you fall.

And when depression and despair shout loudly in my face,

   another voice within me says, "Get up and win that race!"

Olympic Gold medalist J. W. Mashburn. *Courtesy J. W. Mashburn.*

CHAPTER FIVE

J.W. Mashburn, World Class Runner

Jesse William "J.W." Mashburn was born in Seminole, Oklahoma on Valentine's Day in 1933 and soon won the hearts of all of those that followed his storied rise to one of the greatest runners of modern-day times.

His father worked in the oilfields and the family soon moved to Hobbs, New Mexico where Mashburn attended public school and got his first exposure to running competitively while in the 6th grade. Following his completion of the 9th grade his father took a superintendent's job at an oil refinery and moved the family to Wichita Falls, Texas. When his father was killed in a fire at the refinery, he, his mother, and younger brother Berry, moved to Oklahoma City where they had extended family. His mother accepted a job at Tinker Air Force Base and Mashburn enrolled in Capitol Hill High School. It was 1949 and the track program was still in its infancy. A young Coach Vaughn was determined to make it another of Capitol Hill's successful and highly respected sports programs.

"Coach Vaughn promoted the program and did a wonderful job," said Mashburn. "He was very much a disciplinarian. He took my brother and me under his wing as he knew we had lost our father. He was like a father figure to us. He made sure we had some kind of job. I worked for him umpiring baseball games for *The Daily Oklahoman*. He was an idol of mine. I watched him take that program from the ground up. If you wanted to be in that track program, you had to be committed. He did a great job."

"The thing about Coach Vaughn was that he really worked at what he was doing. I have watched high school track teams, and the athletes are pretty much on their own. They are not going through a planned

While at Capitol Hill High School, J. W. Mashburn was a star sprinter and hurdler. *Courtesy J. W. Mashburn.*

organized workout. In all of the different events competitors have to have a different regiment. They have to be trained to their specialty.

"Quarter-milers and sprinters are different. Abe Lemons said that track is the easiest thing to coach. All you do is line them up, tell them to stay to the left, and get back as quick as they can. Everybody knew Coach Vaughn was a good Christian man and it didn't matter what day of the week, Saturday, Sunday, we knew we could go by his house and pick up a key so we could work out. He was always there when we needed him."

When it came to discipline "we all knew that he wasn't going to cope with anything but the best. You didn't miss workouts. If you did you were gone. I never heard him get loud with anybody. He never screamed or hollered, but he demanded respect. He was very fair."

Being new, the track program did not enjoy the status and support equal to the football, basketball, wrestling, and baseball teams. "But once the track team got going all the coaches wanted anyone on their teams to run track if they could. They knew it would help their teams as well," said Mashburn. "When I was introduced to the program, I jumped at the opportunity to run for Coach Vaughn."

In high school, Mashburn's events included the 220-yard dash, 440-yard dash, 180-yard hurdles, 440- and 880-yard relays, and the mile relay. "I have a lot of fond memories of my days at Capitol Hill. I remember that after our junior year, Coach Vaughn arranged for four of us to go to the Junior Olympic meet in Houston, Texas. He didn't go with us but arranged for Dick Woods, Speed Jones, Oscar Shuler, and myself to go. We ran and between the four of us we lacked just one point in winning the whole meet," said Mashburn.

Of the three years that Mashburn ran for Capitol Hill, 1949, 1950, and 1951, the Redskins track team finished with state championships in 1950 and 1951. At his final state high school meet Mashburn ran a 48.1

From left, with Coach Ray Vaughn center, Capitol Hill High School Mile Relay Team members Oscar Shuler, Darrell Smith, Bob Moon, and J.W. Mashburn. *Courtesy J. W. Mashburn.*

second 440 which, at the time, was one-tenth of a second off the American record for the 440.

During his career at Capitol Hill, Mashburn lettered in football, basketball and track; played on the Redskins State Championship Football team in 1949; was a member of back-to-back State Championship Track Teams; won individual state titles in the 180-yard hurdles, 220-yard dash, and 440-yard dash, and ran on championship relay teams in the 440-, 880-, and mile relay.

A GREAT COLLEGIATE AND OLYMPIC TRACK CAREER

Upon graduation from Capitol Hill High School in 1951, Mashburn attended and ran for the University of Oklahoma. However, even as a college freshman his sights were set considerably higher. In 1952 Mashburn traveled to California to participate in the U.S. Olympic trials. "I had never been that far" said Mashburn, "there was no question that was track country. The weather, the schools, the University of Southern California dominated the track and field competition."

Mashburn finished fourth in the 400-meter and qualified for the U.S. 1600-meter Olympic relay team. The night before he was to run in the Summer Olympic Games held in Helsinki, Finland, one of his coaches, Larry Snider, came to his room and said, according to Mashburn, "We are not going to run you because Jamaica has a world class 1600-meter relay that holds the world record in the 1600-, 440-, and half mile. We are fearful that you do not have enough experience, so we are going to put Charlie Moore, a 400-meter hurdler from Cornell, who is a senior, in your place." A July 11, 1976 article in *The Daily Oklahoman* picks up the story with Mashburn reportedly telling his coach: "I think you're making a mistake and I'm

From left, the University of Oklahoma Relay Team of J.W. Mashburn, Quanah Cox, George McCormick, and Harry Lee. *Courtesy J. W. Mashburn.*

going to try to prove it to you every chance I get." Moore, Mashburn's replacement, started his anchor leg with a substantial 17-yard lead; however, the Jamaican runner caught him and won by a stride, setting a new world record, while relegating the U.S. to a silver medal and costing Mashburn an Olympic medal, possibly gold.

The following week Mashburn found himself in London running in the British Empire-US Meet in White City Stadium. Jamaica, a British Empire country, was ready to compete against the U.S. team again, expecting the same outcome experienced in Helsinki. Mashburn recalled that "Larry Snider called me and said 'we want to put you in as anchor.' Even though I was a freshman we, beat them by two steps and set another new world record. The coach told me after the race that they should have run me in the Olympics.

"After my sophomore year at OU I talked to Coach John Jacobs and told him I was leaving OU. My intent was to transfer to the University of Southern California but I discovered that if I did that I would lose a year of

Oklahoma A & M Track Coach Ralph Higgins. *Courtesy Oklahoma State University.*

Oklahoma A & M Track Coach Ralph Higgins times J. W. Mashburn. *Courtesy J. W. Mashburn.*

eligibility. I realized I couldn't do that so I talked to coaches Ralph Higgins and Hank Iba, who said I could transfer to Oklahoma A&M, now Oklahoma State University, without losing any eligibility because at that time Oklahoma A&M was in the Missouri Valley Conference while OU was in the Big Seven."

Mashburn did have to sit out a year when he was a junior, 1953-1954, and didn't run on the A&M track team. He did continue to compete in numerous meets as an independent. He even entered the decathlon competition at the Kansas Relays and won. Returning to competition for Oklahoma A&M in 1954, Mashburn ran under the tutelage of track coach Ralph Higgins. "Coach Higgins was an excellent coach, a lot like Coach Vaughn. A&M was getting ready to build a new track north of the football stadium," said Mashburn.

In 1955, Mashburn's 4x400 relay team won the gold medal in the Pan American Games in Mexico City. He also was the NCAA 400-meter champion that year.

The following year, the Summer Olympic Games were held in Melbourne, Australia. Mashburn once again qualified for the competition by winning his second straight 400-meter NCAA Championship. His memory of that summer's competition focuses more on a "tune up" meet in Hawaii prior to the games. Mashburn and his longtime friend, competitor, and Olympic teammate Jim Lea of USC were there for about a week during which time Mashburn experienced an impacted wisdom tooth. "I never had a dental problem in my life prior to that or since. They had to take me to surgery so there was a question whether I would even get to run or not," Mashburn said. Fortunately, Mashburn quickly recovered. However, Jim Lea tore his Achilles tendon and did not get to run.

When the Olympics began, the U.S. 1600-meter relay team found themselves with only three 400-meter runners and had to substitute Tom Courtney, a half-miler, to fill out the team. This time, the race was significantly less dramatic. Mashburn ran the first leg of the relay, putting the Americans into a solid lead and allowing his teammates to cruise to the gold medal.

Olympians J. W. Mashburn and Jim Lea. *Courtesy J. W. Mashburn.*

After the Olympics, Mashburn returned to Oklahoma City and went to work for Dunlap Sporting Goods. He also stayed in shape by working out on the Oklahoma City Golf & Country Club golf course in preparation for the 1960 Olympic trials. One day, during a workout in 1959, Mashburn tore his Achilles tendon which he says "ended my career. I went all over the country to doctors trying to fix my Achilles. They know how to repair it now, but they couldn't back then. Finally, I had Dr. Clarence Gallagher surgically fix it, but it was years before I could walk or jog on it without it being tender."

Olympic Gold Medalist J. W. Mashburn. *Courtesy J. W. Mashburn.*

LIFE AFTER TRACK

Mashburn remembered, "when I worked at Dunlap's I started selling houses on the weekends out here in south Oklahoma City for a friend of mine. One of my high school classmates, Benny Nall, and I formed a real estate company and started building in 1960. We did our first development over here on a five-acre tract on Walker. We just stuck a street in and a cul-de-sac. Then we did one on Council Road. Benny got the airplane bug, started flying, then moved to Kansas City and opened an airplane operation and did quite well."

While he has built a number of commercial buildings over the years

Following the dedication of the monument honoring J. W. Mashburn, he spent time visiting and reminiscing with those in attendance.

The plaque on the monument honoring J. W. Mashburn, located in Earlywine Park in south Oklahoma City, forever preserves his achievements.

Mashburn has primarily focused on the development of housing additions and residential construction.

When asked if he thought his competition at the highest level of athletic achievement had contributed to his success later in life he answered unequivocally, "I don't think there is any question about it. One of my coaches, it might have been Coach Vaughn, said 'He who thinks he can, can'. I've always remembered that. It is like any other business, it has its ups and downs. We've been through some tough times, we've been through some good times, but you just have to learn to hang in there."

Mashburn is often called on to speak to different groups about his experiences, which he welcomes. His message is simple, "Be honest and treat people the way you want to be treated. Be fair and meet your obligations. Work hard. Nothing takes the place of hard work."

Members from throughout the Oklahoma City community turned out for a surprise unveiling of a monument honoring Olympian J. W. Mashburn in south Oklahoma City's Earlywine Park.

In 2015, Mashburn's contributions as an athlete and as a community leader and contributor were recognized with a surprise unveiling of a monument on the Earlywine Park Walking and Jogging Trail in south Oklahoma City.

THE ATHLETIC AND BUSINESS SUCCESS OF J. W. MASHBURN INCLUDE:

- Graduate of Capitol Hill High School and Oklahoma A&M University
- Member of state high school championship football team in 1949
- Member of state high school championship track and field teams in 1951 and 1952
- Individual state championships in the 180-yard hurdles, 220-yard dash, and 440-yard dash

- Team state championships in the 400-yard, 800-yard and mile relays

- NCAA 400-meter champion in 1955 and 1956

- Member of the US Olympic teams in 1952 and 1956

- Member of the 1952 1600-meter relay team that set a new World Record in London, England

- Gold Medalist in the 1956 Summer Olympics in Melbourne, Australia

- Named NCAA All-American in Track at Oklahoma A&M University, 1955 and 1956

- Named Oklahoma 400-Meter Runner of the Century by *The Daily Oklahoman*, 1999

- Inducted into the Oklahoma Sports Hall of Fame, 2001

- Named the Oklahoma Track Athlete of the Century (1907-2007) by

The Daily Oklahoman

- Prominent real estate developer who, in addition to others, created Sky Ranch, Village Green, Wingspread, Pennsylvania Place, and Cascata Estates additions

- Board of Directors of the 1989 U.S. Olympic Sports Festival

- Member of the Jim Thorpe Hall of Fame Selection Committee

- Vice Chairman of the State Fair of Oklahoma

- Trustee of Oklahoma Industries Authority and the Oklahoma City Metropolitan Area Public Schools Trust

- Inducted into Oklahoma City Public School Wall of Fame, Oklahoma State University Athletic Hall of Honor, and Oklahoma State University Alumni Hall of Fame

- Recipient of prestigious South Oklahoma City Chamber of Commerce Native Son Award, 1997

- Member of the Central Oklahoma Home Builders Association, Southwest Oklahoma Home Builders Association, and National Association of Home Builders

- Board member of the Oklahoma Industries Authority

- President of J.W. Mashburn Development, Inc. and General Partner in Mashburn Land Investment Company, founded in 1960

REMEMBERING COACH VAUGHN
by J.W. MASHBURN

"Coach Vaughn was a great family man and very humble. He was certainly respected as a person and a coach. When I was a sophomore in high school, Coach Vaughn taught me not only running techniques, but discipline too. He encouraged me daily by telling me 'You have the ability to go as far in the track world as you want, you just have to work for it.'

Olympic Gold medalist and Oklahoma City businessman J. W. Mashburn.

Coach Vaughn always treated me like a son and encouraged me to set high goals. This meant so much to me since I had lost my father when I was 15. My mother was working to support me and my brother, Berry, so money was tight. Coach would find me 'paying' jobs in the summer. I refereed little league games and watered the football field at Capitol Hill. I truly feel that Coach Vaughn was a major contributor to any success I have had in track."

Coach Ray Vaughn.

CHAPTER SIX

A Lifelong Commitment to Christian Education

In 1946, shortly after the end of World War II and roughly 13 years following the closure of Cordell Christian College, there was considerable interest among the members of the church of Christ to reopen a Christian college in Oklahoma. After four years of discussion and planning, the effort resulted in the opening of Central Christian College in Bartlesville, Oklahoma in 1950.

To learn more about the history of Oklahoma Christian University, the following are excellent resources. *Central Christian College: From Dream to Reality* by W. O. Beeman, *Jubilee* by J. Terry Johnson, and *Soaring on Wings Like Eagles, A History of Oklahoma Christian University* by Dr. Stafford North.

Ultimately, seven years of operation in Bartlesville resulted in the decision by the board of trustees to move the school to Oklahoma City in order to grow. With the assistance of the Oklahoma City Chamber of Commerce, the board secured 200 acres of land on the northern border of the Oklahoma City metropolitan area and broke ground on a modern, newly-designed college campus. The campus was located on the north side of Memorial Road between Eastern and Bryant avenues in north Oklahoma City. The college was renamed Oklahoma Christian College in 1959 and earned university status in 1990.

One of the original classroom buildings on the campus of Central Christian College. *Courtesy Oklahoma Christian* Aerie.

Coach Ray Vaughn relaxing in his Capitol Hill home. *Courtesy Oklahoma Christian* Aerie.

Realizing the importance of a solid athletic program, the school's second president, Dr. James O. Baird, approached Capitol Hill High School Athletic Director and Track Coach Ray Vaughn to join the faculty of Central Christian College as the school's athletic director in order to establish basketball and track programs at the new institution.

It must have been an exciting opportunity for the young coach whose father, years earlier, had devoted himself and his family to the operation of Cordell Christian College. Yet, as the athletic director of one of the city's largest and most successful athletic programs, along with a seemingly endless supply of quality athletes, his future and job security at Capitol Hill High School must have likewise been difficult to leave.

Yet, leave he did, spending the balance of his life devoted to the growth and success of what is today Oklahoma Christian University and even more importantly, many would argue, the student athletes that he

Coach Ray Vaughn in his first office on the campus of Central Christian College. *Courtesy Oklahoma Christian* Aerie.

Basketball games were played in northwest Oklahoma City's Casady High School Gymnasium until the new college could build its own facility. *Courtesy Oklahoma Christian* Aerie.

coached for the next 22 years.

Coach Vaughn's first year of coaching at Central Christian College began in the fall of 1958 with much excitement, opportunity, and promise. What the school did not have that year, or the year thereafter, was anything that resembled athletic facilities. Imagine trying to recruit college athletes in basketball and track without a gymnasium or track oval on which to compete.

With no gymnasium in which to practice or play games, the inaugural basketball squad made use of the Casady High School facilities in northwest Oklahoma City, roughly 10 miles southwest of the college campus. Remarkably, given the facilities issues, Coach Vaughn's Eagle basketball team finished the season with a winning record of 15-8, including victories over Central State College from Edmond and Shawnee's Oklahoma Baptist and St. Gregory's.

A large metal building was constructed on the campus in 1960.

Dubbed "The Barn" for obvious reasons, it contained a basketball court, bleacher seating for around 600, dressing rooms, a coach's office, and public restrooms. That year, having a gym they could call their own gave the Eagles a "home field' advantage resulting in a season record of 24-2. The starting five players on the team that year

Coach Ray Vaughn beams with pride outside The Barn, the new athletic facilities on the Central Christian College campus. *Courtesy Oklahoma Historical Society.*

included Dennis McMasters, Robert Watson, Jim Miller, and two Arkansas Tech transfers—brothers James and Frank Davis.

The college was not only growing in athletic acuity, but academically as well. What had started in Oklahoma City in 1958 as a "junior college," already had progressed to the point that it could transition to full "senior college" status in the fall of 1962.

Coach Vaughn recruited players with obvious athletic talent; however, he also considered a player's character and spirituality with the understanding that they would reflect on the reputation of the school for which they competed. An entry in the 1960 Central Christian College yearbook, the *Aerie*, states, "Even though he wants to win in the events, he considers honesty, fair play, and true Christian behavior more important. He is concerned with each individual boy and hopes that participation in athletics in a Christian atmosphere will build strong character."

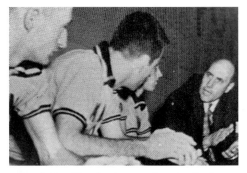

Coach Ray Vaughn instructing the Eagles basketball team. *Courtesy Oklahoma Christian* Aerie.

Vaughn coached varsity basketball only during the school's first four years in Oklahoma City, relinquishing that role to a number of successors. However, while coaching basketball, he amassed an impressive record of 64 wins against only 24 losses.

FULL-TIME TRACK AND FIELD COACH

As the newly-hired Haskell Sinclair, an Abilene Christian College graduate, took over as the full-time basketball coach in 1962, Vaughn concentrated on his athletic director and track coaching duties. With the new gymnasium in place it was time to begin thinking about a track and field complex. At this point, the Oklahoma Christian College Booster Club stepped in, with the assistance of others, and built the school its first track with a red cinder running surface. The program was expanded that same year to include a cross country team.

During Vaughn's 22 years at Oklahoma Christian, as its head track coach and athletic director, hundreds

The new red cinder track was constructed on the campus in 1962. *Courtesy Randy Heath.*

of athletes donned the maroon and gray of the Oklahoma Christian Track Team. Many had outstanding careers, leaving unbroken records, heralded accounts of athletic achievement, and stories of success, not only on the field of competition, but off as well. The following is a chronological list of a few of their highlights, photos, and their own first-person accounts of their experiences and memories of their longtime coach.

Early Oklahoma Christian College maroon and gray track uniforms.

1966

Richard "Dickie" Gray, a long jumper from Florence, Alabama, became the school's first NAIA All-American with a leap of 24 feet and 9 inches.

1967

The 880-yard relay team of Richard "Dickie" Gray, Roscoe Cogburn, Larry Rehl, and Harold "Hal" Ballou set a new school record of 1:25.24. As of 2016, the record had not been broken.

Larry Rehl, Roscoe Cogburn, Harold "Hal" Ballou, and Jim Butler set a new school record in the mile relay with a 3:11.32, a mark that has not been bested since.

Newcomer, freshman Jeff Bennett, posted significant wins in

Oklahoma Christian College's Jeff Bennett easily clears the bar in the pole vault. *Courtesy Oklahoma Christian* Aerie.

national competition in the pole vault and the 400-meter hurdles.

1968

Jeff Bennett captured a national title taking first place in the 400-meter hurdles with a time of 51.44 becoming Oklahoma Christian's second All-American.

1969

Vaughn turned over coaching duties for the Oklahoma Christian cross country program to assistant coach Randy Heath.

1970

Jeff Bennett and fellow decathlete Gary Hill, won first and third, respectively, at the Kansas and Drake Relays. Bennett's Drake Relay score of 8,072, in the decathlon, remains the third-highest score nationally and set a

Assistant Coach Randy Heath. *Courtesy Oklahoma Christian* Aerie.

Decathlete Jeff Bennett, far right, wins the first NAIA Decathlon Title ever awarded. Gary Hill, third from right, placed third nationally. *Courtesy Oklahoma Christian* Aerie.

new Oklahoma Christian record.

Coach Ray Vaughn is picked by the U.S. Olympic Committee to coach Olympic decathlete candidates in Colorado Springs, Colorado, as they prepare for the Olympic Games in Munich, Germany.

Gene Grassie took second in the NAIA Outdoor Nationals in the javelin throw. Grassie also set a new school record in the old-rule javelin with a throw of 241 feet and 10 inches.

1971

Vaughn returned to Colorado Springs to work with Olympic decathlete hopefuls looking forward to the Olympic trials and games the following year.

1972

Jeff Bennett makes the U.S. Olympic team in the Decathlon and competed in the Olympic Games in Munich, Germany finishing fourth in the competition and first among all American contenders.

The Oklahoma Christian Track and Field Team finished fourth out of 123 colleges in the NAIA National Track Meet.

Gary Hill won the national title in the Decathlon achieving All-

American status.

Jim Neugent won the national title in the hammer throw, as well as the discus along with All-American recognition. As of 2016, Neugent still held school records in the shot put, discus, and hammer throw.

Gary Hill clears the pole vault bar during preparation for the national meet in the decathlon. *Courtesy Oklahoma Christian Aerie.*

Dale Paas scored a second place finish at the national meet in the two-mile race walk along with All-American honors.

1973

Coach Vaughn is asked to manage the United States AAU track team in a dual meet against Russia in Moscow giving Oklahoma Christian and its head track coach international experience and exposure.

1976

Bobby Boswell became Oklahoma Christian's first cross country All-American by finishing eleventh in the NAIA National Meet.

1977

The distance medley relay team, comprised of Gary Tatum, Bobby Smith, Ron Stangeland, and Steve Wolfe, finished first at the NAIA National Track Meet with a time of 10:01.00.

From left, Oklahoma Christian Relay Team Ron Stangeland, Bobby Smith, Wayne Long, and Steve Wolfe. *Courtesy Oklahoma Christian* Aerie.

Wayne Long placed second in the 600-yard run with a time of 1:11.36. Ron Stangeland took second in the 1,000-yard run with a time of 2:10.33. Bob Bayless placed third in the high jump at 6'7".

The two-mile relay team featuring Gary Tatum, Bobby Smith, Steve Wolfe, and Pat Becher, finished third in a time of 7:47.97. Tom Story follows Boswell's performance the prior year by gaining All-American honors at the NAIA National Cross Country Meet with a twenty-third place finish.

Oklahoma Christian posted its highest finish at the national cross country meet to date, placing fifth out of the 49 schools that qualified. The Oklahoma Christian Eagle track team:

- Won five invitational meets
- Won the District 9 title
- Won the Texoma Conference Meet
- Finished the national indoor track meet, tied for second place, the highest finish ever for an Oklahoma Christian team,
- Was number 13 out of 71 teams at the NAIA National Outdoor. Meet, resulting in Coach Vaughn's best year for team performance for both indoor and outdoor during his Oklahoma Christian career.

1978

Bob Bayless won the NAIA National High Jump title with a 6'10" performance. All-American honors are bestowed on Gary Tatum, Ron Love, Tom Story, and Bobby Smith for their first place finish in the Distance Medley Relay with a time of 10:12.52.

Danny Neugent became an All-American with a third place throw of 174'4" in the hammer throw at the Outdoor National Meet in Abilene, Texas.

The Indoor Two-Mile Relay team of Gary Tatum, Ron Love, Tom Story, and Bobby Smith

Oklahoma Christian All-American high jumper Bob Bayless. *Courtesy Oklahoma Christian* Aerie.

scored a third-place win nationally with a time of 7:44.63.

The Oklahoma Christian Cross Country Team finished the national meet in ninth place.

1979

Coach Ray Vaughn's last year as head track coach at Oklahoma Christian.

Mike Herndon achieved All-American status with a sixth place finish in the National Cross Country Meet, the highest finish ever achieved by an Oklahoma Christian runner. Herndon also won three more All-American titles in the indoor two-mile run, outdoor three-mile run, and the steeplechase.

Oklahoma Christian placed 7th overall out of 43 teams that score at the NAIA Indoor Nationals with 25 points. The Distance Medley Relay and the two-mile relay, both comprised of Gary Tatum, Tom Snider, Tom Story, and Bobby Smith won the national title at the NAIA Indoor Meet.

Bob Bayless took fourth in the 60-yard high hurdles with a time of 7.62.

Mike Herndon captured 6th place with a 14:18.00 finish in the three-mile run.

Oklahoma Christian Athletic Director Ray Vaughn relinquished his title of head coach of the track and field team to student, athlete, friend, colleague, and assistant coach Randy Heath.

Athletic Director Ray Vaughn and newly-named head coach Randy Heath discuss the daily workout schedule for the Oklahoma Christian track team. *Courtesy Oklahoma Christian* Aerie.

In Vaughn's 22-year career at Oklahoma Christian he saw 60 of his athletes achieve the honor of All-Americans.

BASKETBALL STAR AND COACH

Coach Frank Davis remembered, "When Coach Vaughn recruited my brother James and me to play basketball at Central Christian College, we didn't even have a gymnasium in which to play. That finally got built the first year we were at Oklahoma Christian, just as he told us it would. That gym became Coach Vaughn's home away from home. It was a short walk from his house, which was just across the pasture, from the gym, and near his fishing pond. When I played for Coach Vaughn and later when I was sharing the only office in the gym with Max

Basketball Coach Frank Davis talks about his memories of The Barn. *Courtesy Oklahoma Christian* Aerie.

Dobson and Coach Vaughn, we took care of the basics in that old barn. When they brought the bleachers in to be installed, Ray Vaughn, myself, and my teammates set those bleachers up for the first time. That became our responsibility from then on. Coach Vaughn was the man in charge of making sure that everything was ready for each event. It soon became part

An early photo of The Barn, the home of Oklahoma Christian's early-day athletic program. *Courtesy Oklahoma Christian* Aerie.

of the family, and because of the simple inexpensive structure and shape the students dubbed it 'The Barn.'

"We all took pride in the fact that almost everything in those days was simple. Kids can turn something plain and unimpressive into a thing of pride. That's what we did as part of our motivation to become something special. The clatter of boards being put into place and the sound of the framework for the bleachers screeching across the concrete floor still sounds in my memory. The sight of players working urgently and Coach Vaughn moving from one end of the bleachers to the other, putting boards in place, and giving instructions to his boys, is a family image that will never fade from my memory.

"He did his turn walking side by side with players pushing those big wide floor mops up and down the gym floor, making it shine like new money in advance of our teams hitting the floor to play that night. I never was aware of Coach Vaughn's background at the time.

"With only a faith and conviction to do something special, he had given up being the athletic director of the most powerful athletic program at the biggest and best high school in Oklahoma, to become the only coach and athletic director at an unknown little college, with a few new buildings, on the highest point in an open

Wooden bleachers inside The Barn would accommodate the entire student body and fans of early basketball games. *Courtesy Oklahoma Christian* Aerie.

Coach Ray Vaughn taking a time-out in the home locker room of The Barn. *Courtesy Oklahoma Historical Society.*

200-acre pasture. So, there he was, setting up bleachers for his team, sweeping the floors, sharing his office with his dog, Pal. No wonder he became our inspiration and hope. We followed such a man. Our lives were dramatically made better as a consequence. That old barn saw some of the best teams in the country come calling, only to lose. They were Oral Roberts University, Abilene Christian University, Oklahoma Baptist University, Oklahoma City University, and Midwestern University, just to name a few; and under his leadership those teams, who set up bleachers, over time played such teams as New Mexico State University, University of Texas at El Paso, University of Arkansas, and Memphis State University.

"That old barn was shared by all the sports teams. I remember our practices in basketball when I was the coach, the shot putters would practice at one end, and Jeff Bennett practiced his pole vault in a vaulting pit set up along the side of the court. Jeff was preparing for the Olympics. We had to share that old barn. We were a team in every way. We weren't too proud to share. We had a perfect example to follow, in Coach Ray Vaughn. I wish I could do it all over again."

In 1991 Frank Davis was among the first three inductees into the Oklahoma Christian University Athletic Hall of Fame. Davis was a record setting basketball player and ultimately head coach of the Oklahoma Christian Basketball Team during his career. He was inducted by then Athletic Director, Max Dobson, along with Raymond Vaughn and Jeff Bennett.

Coach Frank Davis, with his wife Judy, was honored as one of the first inductees into the Oklahoma Christian Athletic Hall of Fame. He was presented for induction by Oklahoma Christian Athletic Director Max Dobson. *Courtesy Oklahoma Christian University.*

A FACELIFT FOR
THE OLD BARN

After fifty years of faithful service, The Barn received a needed update through the application of a new coat of paint and the restoration of the hardwood basketball court. The facility was rededicated on November 6, 2010 during a special homecoming event known as the "Barn Bash" which has continued at each homecoming since. The beloved facility was renamed in honor of its benefactor and is now known as the "Dave Smith

The Barn at Oklahoma Christian received a facelift thanks to the generosity of former Eagle Basketball player Dave Smith.

Updates to The Barn included a newly-renovated court.

Athletic Center—The Barn".

A SHIP WITHOUT A RUDDER

That's how Oklahoma Christian's first All-American describes himself. Richard "Dickie" Gray had a tough start in life. His father was an alcoholic that abandoned him and his mother, leaving them to fend for themselves in Florence, Alabama. His mother had finished the 5th grade, his father the 6th. The best thing Dickie had going for him was the gifts that God had given him. He could run and he could jump.

Oklahoma Christian Long Jumper Dickie Gray was the school's first All-American. *Courtesy Oklahoma Christian Aerie.*

As a high school student, Dickie led the state in scoring on his basketball team and had a 23-foot long jump on the track team. When he summarized his athletic achievements in a letter to Coach Vaughn he received a full scholarship offer from Central Christian. When he got to the small school's campus in Oklahoma City he said, "While I was a Christian I really thought of myself as a derelict. Coach Vaughn taught me so much. He got me focused. He gave me a reason to train and to work. He was the only positive role model in my life. As a result, I wanted to be just like him. I majored in education with plans to become a track and field coach."

Dickie related that in one of his fatherly moments Coach Vaughn made an unusual request of the All-American athlete. "Let me smell your fingers Dickie," said the coach. After doing so, Coach Vaughn's response to the finger smelling was, "Dickie, you've got to quit smoking." Dickie reported that, at least for a while, "I didn't quit smoking, but I did start washing my hands better."

Upon graduation from Oklahoma Christian Dickie began teaching and coaching at Jefferson Junior High in Oklahoma City. He also worked on a truck dock at night to supplement his income. His wife, Judy, whom he met and married in Tennessee, was a stenographer for the local office of the Federal Bureau of Investigation and Dickie often interacted and played basketball with the local FBI agents. One day one of the agents mentioned to Dickie that the FBI was recruiting new agents and that he should apply. He says his first response was, "I don't want to get shot." After being assured that being shot was highly unlikely, he took the entrance exams, passed his physical, and became an FBI agent.

In his more than 29 years with the bureau, Agent Richard Gray has been assigned to FBI offices in Oklahoma City, Milwaukee, Baltimore and Memphis. During that time, Dickie was faithful to his country and faithful to his God. While in Memphis he not only taught Sunday and Wednesday night Bible classes, but he was also asked to be a Deacon in his church, ministering to the disadvantaged and underprivileged. When he was appointed as a Deacon the first person he called to tell about it was his old college coach. "He was the most important man in my life," says Dickie, "Whenever something good happened to me Coach Vaughn was the first to know."

Agent Gray is now comfortably retired and living on the Gulf Coast with his wife Judy with whom he recently celebrated over 51 years of marriage. They have two grown sons who have been the beneficiary of a positive male role model in their lives. Dickie

Former FBI Agent, Richard "Dickie" Gray and his wife Judy. *Courtesy Dickie Gray.*

Gray has achieved a lot in his life including one of his goals upon arriving at Oklahoma Christian, he is a lot like his old college coach.

"HONESTLY, I'M A LITTLE NERVOUS COACH"

Harold "Hal" Ballou was the fastest quarter-miler on the Oklahoma Christian Track Team; however, his team was at the Texas Relays and Coach Vaughn had asked him to run the 440-yard hurdles, a race that he had never run before. It was almost time to leave for the track and he was alone in his room when the coach knocked on his door and asked if he was ready.

"Honestly, I'm a little nervous coach," was Hal's reply. At that point Coach Vaughn simply said "Let's pray about it". Hal remembers, "I wasn't a Christian then, but I said OK. Coach Vaughn grabbed my hand and prayed that I would be ready for the race, that all my skills would be sharp, and that I would be able to do the best I could. Chills went all over me. I will never forget that. It certainly made an impression on me."

"I looked at him with a different set of eyes after that" says Ballou, "I'd run any race he asked me to."

Hal came in third in his race that day; however, his time set a new school record for the event which lasted until newcomer Jeff Bennett broke Hal's record a few years later.

Hal also recalls that in the early days, around the early to mid-sixties, the team would travel to meets in a couple of station wagons and that when it was time to eat, Coach Vaughn would pull into a restaurant and tell us to wait in the car until he went in and made sure they could feed us. Sometimes he would come out and announce that they could take care of us and sometimes he would get back in the car and say we were going to push on down the road a little before we stopped. We had a number of black athletes on our team. It did not occur to me until much later that Coach Vaughn was making sure that all of our teammates would be welcome before he let any of us get out of the car and that if not, we would keep driving until we found a place that did.

Hal Ballou, left, and Roscoe Cogburn cross the finish line taking first and second in the 440-yard dash. *Courtesy Oklahoma Christian* Aerie.

Hal became a Christian while at Oklahoma Christian and met and married his wife Mary Beth. They celebrated their 52nd wedding anniversary in 2016.

Coach Vaughn and Hal Ballou at the Ballou Wedding. *Courtesy Hal Ballou.*

Harold and Mary Beth Ballou. *Courtesy Hal Ballou.*

OKLAHOMA CHRISTIAN'S "ALSO RAN"

Forrest Reed was a new high school graduate from Konawa, Oklahoma who was entered in the 440- at his state meet but he had a false start and was disqualified from the competition. As a result, he had no "times" in state competition with which to attract scholarship offers. He was

a Christian and very interested in attending Oklahoma Christian. His high school coach took him to a college AAU meet that summer at which Oklahoma Christian had a team competing. He ran the 440- finishing somewhere in the "back of the pack." Coach Vaughn, however, was interested enough to offer him a half scholarship if he could come up with the rest of the tuition. Forrest recounts, "On a handshake, he literally

Quarter-miler Forrest Reed earned his spot on the mile relay every week and he benefited from the competition. *Courtesy Forrest Reed.*

changed my life. He put me into an environment that strengthened my spiritual being and into contact with great people that prepared me for life that I would never have met without him taking a chance on me. He provided me with constant leadership and encouragement."

Forrest says he did not have enough talent to be a star in any one event so he always ran in the relays. He remembers, "We had three fast guys, Hal Ballou, Roscoe Cogburn, and Jim Butler. Then we had three or four guys that had to run 'time trials' every Thursday to see who was going to be the fourth member of that mile relay team that set so many records in the late '60's. I was always that guy running for the fourth spot.

"We ran in a meet in Lubbock, Texas one weekend and they had several heats running the 440-yard dash. I wasn't scheduled to run that race, but Coach Vaughn asked me to run in the slowest heat in hopes that if I could win it would mean an extra point for the team. When they introduced the race they named all of the runners until they got to my lane and the announcer said 'also running in lane 6, Oklahoma Christian'. As a result, my teammates began to call me 'Also Ran'. The good news was that I won the heat and a point for my team."

As a reminder of how the small things in our lives often give us

Coach Vaughn, third from right, talks to members of his relay team, from left, Ralph Charlton, Ed Harless, Forrest Reed, Hal Ballou, and Roscoe Cogburn. *Courtesy Oklahoma Christian University.*

direction and control our destiny, Forrest stated that, "After my career at Oklahoma Christian, Ron Baker, one of my acquaintances from school, was coaching in Joplin, Missouri. He called me one day and said his school needed a math teacher that could coach track. He knew that was my career training and I got the job. I taught and coached for fifteen years in Joplin and worked on my Master's Degree in mathematics and computer science. The only way I knew to coach was the way Coach taught me through his example. As a result, I was proud to produce three Missouri State Champion track teams. I left coaching and spent twenty years working for a defense contractor as their vice president of quality assurance for aerospace applications. I seriously doubt any of the successes I have enjoyed in life would have occurred had Coach Vaughn not taken a chance on a mediocre kid from Konawa and put me on a path that provided my wife and I with a wonderful life." Forrest Reed met his wife Christine at Oklahoma Christian and has been married more than 50 years.

"SOMEONE MAY BE GOING HOME ON THE NEXT BUS"

Gary Hill and Jim Neugent met their freshman year at Oklahoma Christian. They soon found that they had more in common than their track scholarships and a keen interest in competition. The best friends quickly bonded and thrived under the oversight of Coach Vaughn.

Gary remembered, "We were in White Oak, Texas for the first outdoor meet of the season. Our rooms were next to each other on the second floor of the hotel above the swimming pool. There was a small

Best friends and teammates, Gary Hill left, and Jim Neugent. *Courtesy Oklahoma Christian* Aerie.

ledge right outside the window between our rooms. Always looking for an opportunity to sharpen our skills, Neugent and I decided to see if we could roll a sixteen-pound shot up and down the ledge between our windows. Not long after our successful execution of that challenge Coach Vaughn called a team meeting. With the whole team in attendance, the coach discussed the possibility of someone going home on the next bus and that we were there to compete and always to do what was right. Everybody else on the team had puzzled looks on their faces. Only Neugent and I knew what he was talking about. Needless to say, Jim and I always tried to do what was right after that."

Jim Neugent with his sixteen pound shot. He still holds the school record. *Courtesy Oklahoma Christian* Aerie.

QUIT CRYING AND START COMPETING

"My junior year at the national meet," Gary Hill said, "I was complaining and whining about some small matter. Finally, Coach Vaughn had enough and told me to quit crying and start competing. It was some of the best advice I ever received.

"After graduating and becoming a coach I tried to pattern myself along his lines of encouragement and techniques. Not only was Coach Vaughn a great coach, he was a better man and a tremendous friend."

"A CHAMPION WILL PERFORM"

Jim Neugent was a "footballer" and "wrestler" at Capitol Hill High School, but he also was a "thrower". He threw the shot put and the discus. Jim's track coach at Capitol Hill just happened to be Jim King, who had thrown the shot and discus at Oklahoma Christian for Coach Vaughn.

Although Neugent admits that he was small for the throwing events, Vaughn gave him a scholarship based on King's recommendation. "I couldn't have gone to school any other way," Neugent said. "Coach Vaughn's methods of coaching were totally different than anything I had experienced in high school. He would always furnish whatever you needed, but he expected you to do the work. He never raised his voice. He could get more across without speaking

Jim Neugent throwing the discus. In 2016, he still held the Oklahoma Christian school record. *Courtesy Oklahoma Christian* Aerie.

a word than most people could ranting and raving. He would give you everything you needed to know about your event but you were the one that had to do it. He was an unbelievable motivator as far as I was concerned."

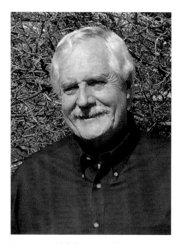

Former Oklahoma Christian All-American Race Walker Dale Paas. *Courtesy Dale Paas.*

contacted me with great encouragement that through his program I could succeed in track and get a college degree at the same time. He gave me the chance to excel in track where I would have only been mediocre at the other more traditional sports.

"As a runner at OC, I had a place to fit in and a group to identify with. When Coach Vaughn suggested that I take up race walking, I had never even heard of the event. Through his encouragement and support I was able to do well in the 'weird event' and at the same time stay in school long enough to get a degree. Coach Vaughn cultivated an atmosphere of goal setting and success that has helped me throughout the years of my life."

The event of "race walking" is generally a long distance foot race which differs from running in that at least one foot must remain in touch with the ground at all times. Dale Paas was a two time NAIA All-American in the two-mile race walk, placing second nationally in 1972 and again in 1973.

Dale Paas, center, was a race walker before most people knew what the event was. *Courtesy Oklahoma Christian* Aerie.

SHEER STRENGTH HAS ITS BENEFIT

Mike McDonald was one of those guys that you could not help but like or laugh at depending on the circumstances. Born and raised in Wichita, Kansas, he enrolled at Oklahoma Christian in 1967 as a business management major. Mike was one of the original "Nine Noises"—nine guys that provided crowd enthusiasm at basketball games through stupid antics—which gave him a ready-made opportunity to display his natural "wise-guy" personality.

Mike McDonald could throw the javelin, but he did not know it. *Courtesy Oklahoma Christian* Aerie.

As was his practice, Coach Vaughn was always on the lookout for athletic talent, especially if that talent was already on campus. One day while he was watching one of the many intramural softball games he noticed Mike playing one of the outfield positions. At that time, the softball field did not have an outfield fence, so when the batter hit the ball over Mike's head he immediately turned and chased it until he caught up with it. What happened next caught Coach Vaughn's eye and changed Mike's life forever.

When Mike picked up the ball he simply turned and threw the ball directly to home plate in time for the catcher to tag the runner out and end the inning. When the game was over, Coach Vaughn approached Mike and

Mike McDonald had a very strong arm. Coach Vaughn re-directed his attention from the softball field to track and field. *Courtesy Oklahoma Christian Aerie.*

Dr. Michael "Mike" Herndon found a new sport at Oklahoma Christian and basketball was not it. In 2016, he served as Chief Medical Officer for the Oklahoma Health Care Authority. *Courtesy Mike Herndon.*

asked if he had ever thought about throwing the javelin. Mike replied "no."

After a few throwing tips from the coach he was on the track team as the school's new javelin thrower.

Mike had great success with his new found talent and ranked second on Oklahoma Christian's all-time list for the "old-rule" javelin with a throw of 236'-3" at Winfield, Kansas in 1971.

A TREMENDOUS ATHLETE
IN THE WRONG SPORT

Mike Herndon was a fourth grader in Asher, Oklahoma when he got his first taste of Oklahoma Christian athletics as he and his family attended a basketball game in The Barn. His father was a gospel preacher in Asher and the combination of basketball and Bible study appealed to the ten-year-old.

His completion of high school was complicated somewhat by attending four different schools in his last four years prior to graduation, ultimately graduating from Porter, Oklahoma. The one consistency through that period of time was that he wanted to attend Oklahoma Christian University and play basketball for the Eagles.

Oklahoma Christian head basketball coach Jerry Jobe welcomed the 6', 148-pound point guard to the varsity basketball team, wondering what kind of player he would make. It did not take Jobe long to figure out that Herndon was a good runner, but not such a great basketball player. He talked to Coach Vaughn and shared his thoughts about Mike's basketball skills with the caveat, "but, you should see him run."

Four time All-American, Mike Herndon clears the steeple jump during practice on the Oklahoma Christian track. *Courtesy Oklahoma Christian Aerie.*

Once the basketball season was over Coach Vaughn invited Mike out to the track to see what he could do. Herndon had never run track before, but following a couple of weeks work with the distance runners was able to produce a respectable 4:29 in the mile while also breaking 16 minutes in the three-mile race.

Herndon remembered his next conversation with Coach Vaughn went something like this. "He put his arm around me and told me I ran well. He said, 'I'm going to take you on Mike. I'll give you a full track scholarship on the condition that you give up basketball.'" When Mike sought the advice of Coach Jobe as to the generous offer, he says, "Coach Jobe told me to take the money and run." After that he was a track man.

Mike recalled that one of Coach Vaughn's cross country "catch phrases" was "Work the uphill, use the downhill." He says what that meant was to not slow down

A young Mike Herndon with his cross country coach, Randy Heath.
Courtesy Oklahoma Christian Aerie.

on the uphill climbs and use your energy to pass runners that do and to rest and hold your position on the downhill. He said it worked and it did.

Once again, Coach Vaughn's instincts proved to be spot on. In 1979, Mike Herndon had the highest individual finish of any Oklahoma Christian runner in the national cross country meet gaining All-American honors with a sixth place finish. Later that season, Herndon won three additional All-American honors in the mile, three-mile, and steeplechase, resulting in top honors in four individual events.

While Mike Herndon credits a lot of his success to his cross country coach Randy Heath, he quickly adds that "I wouldn't have had a shot at anything that I've accomplished had it not been for Coach Vaughn's willingness to believe in me."

Randy Health remembers, "I first met Coach Vaughn when I was around eleven years old. My family and the Vaughn family attended the Hillcrest Church of Christ in south Oklahoma City. Coach Vaughn had already resigned his position at Capitol Hill to take the job at Central Christian College. I asked him once what sport he liked the best and he said he really enjoyed basketball, but the individual accomplishment in track and field was very special as well.

"Coach Vaughn's son, Ray, was a year younger than me and a year older than my younger brother Tommy, who now coaches the Oklahoma Christian Women's Softball Team and for whom the OC field is named.

The Vaughn family lived on an acreage that backed up to Lightning Creek on Southwest 50th Street. It was a great place for boys to play and also served as a natural setting for Halloween parties and 'Snipe' hunts.

"For a few years, Coach Vaughn commuted to the new school in far north Oklahoma City; however, he ultimately sold their south side home and moved the family to a 40-acre tract of land adjacent to

Randy Heath became Oklahoma Christian's second head coach of track and field in 1979.

the college campus near Edmond. In the meantime, my family moved to Jacksonville, Florida in the summer of 1963, during my junior year, and I began to run cross country and track and played basketball and baseball.

"That year I ran a 4:41.0 mile and contacted Coach Vaughn about attending OC and he told me that if I could get my time down to 4:30 then he could offer me a partial scholarship after high school graduation. During my senior year I concentrated more on the mile and that paid

Coach Vaughn and his young Oklahoma Christian Letterman protégé Randy Heath. *Courtesy Oklahoma Christian* Aerie.

off when I placed third in a regional meet with a time of 4:29.2 and qualified for the state meet. I wrote the coach and sent him my results. He seemed very pleased with my improvement and offered me a tuition scholarship to run cross country and track for OC, which I thankfully accepted.

"During my freshman year at Oklahoma Christian, I realized that Coach Vaughn had an outstanding reputation on as well as off campus. He was very professional in his teaching and coaching. While at Oklahoma Christian I ran cross country for three seasons, played baseball for three seasons, and ran track for two seasons. In the spring of 1969 Coach Vaughn asked me what I was going to do after graduation. I told him I wanted to teach math and maybe coach. Coach Vaughn said if I could get a teaching job close to Oklahoma Christian he would like for me to come back and help him with the program. I was very surprised and excited about the opportunity to work for him. He wanted me to coach the cross country team and assist him with the track and field team.

"I was hired by the Oklahoma City Public School system to teach math at Eisenhower Junior High School which is only three miles from the Oklahoma Christian Campus. I could actually teach my classes and still get to Oklahoma Christian several minutes early so that Coach and I could discuss that day's workout. I always enjoyed being around him because I could ask him all kinds of questions about coaching and teaching.

"In my first year of teaching, I met Barbara Epley, an education major at OC from Dallas, Texas. Barbara and I married in 1970. It takes a very special person to be the wife of a teacher and coach. Barbara was the special person that I wanted to share my life with. After we married we took many weekend trips with Coach Vaughn and his wife Sue for track and field meets and other events.

Randy and Barbara Heath.

"I coached cross country and assisted Coach Vaughn from 1969 through 1977. He would pay me for nine months out of the year out of his own salary. The extra money helped our family budget a great deal during that eight-year stretch. I had a great experience working for Coach Vaughn."

"Coach Vaughn delegated many responsibilities to me that gave me a great deal of experience at a young age. Coach Vaughn also introduced me to many important people at OC, the College Church of Christ, and many coaches in the NAIA and NCAA that knew him well and greatly respected him.

Some of the duties Randy Heath was assigned while coaching at Oklahoma Christian included:

1. Servicing the Lettermen's Club soda machine in the gym lobby with products, counting the money, and receipting it weekly.

2. Operating the basketball and baseball concession stands during home games and tournaments.

3. Supervising the laundry room for track and field uniforms and practice gear.

4. Assisting with meetings, projects, and functions of the Athletic Booster Club

5. Coordinating the track and field results and brochures.

6. Sponsoring many AAU Junior Olympic age group track and field meets.

"Through the influence of Coach Vaughn I was hired fulltime in 1977 by OC to teach physical education, coach cross country, assist with track and field, and supervise the athletic work-study program. This was a great blessing to me and my family. I realized that Coach Vaughn developed and prepared me to be his successor when it was his time to retire from OC.

One of the other jobs that Randy Heath "learned" was striping the lanes on the old red cinder track. *Courtesy Randy Heath.*

"Coach Vaughn developed many outstanding track and field athletes at OC from 1961 to 1979. He was on the cutting edge of training for new and different events at the time such as the decathlon, javelin, hammer throw, and the race walk. Coach Vaughn retired as the head coach after the 1979 outdoor season. His plans included being the athletic director and professor in the physical education department. OC named me the new head track and field coach for the 1979-1980 school year. Coach Vaughn left me a very talented and experienced team. I realized from the very beginning that I was following a true legend in coaching track and field.

"I knew he was looking forward to helping me in my first year of coaching, however, he was stricken by a brain tumor that was surgically removed in late 1979. He was left partially paralyzed and could not speak. He did his best to spend some time in his office each week; however, once school was out that spring he remained at home.

"In late May of 1980, I took the OC track and field team by his house to see him. We were able to spend about thirty minutes with him before we departed for the NAIA Outdoor National Meet in Abilene, Texas. This was the team that he had recruited and coached for several years before he retired. This was the last time he would see a large group of men that he had coached.

"Many of his former athletes attended his funeral in the fall of 1980. I was honored to be selected as one of his pallbearers by the family. To my regret, I completed my first year as the head coach without the mentoring of Coach Vaughn. I knew Ray Vaughn very well as my coach, teacher, and Christian leader for the four years I attended OC. I knew him even better on a professional level as his assistant coach for ten years as we worked together daily, attended track and field meets on Saturdays, and attended church together on Sundays.

In the Summer of 2015 Coach Randy Heath retired and turned the program over to another former Oklahoma Christian trackman, Wade Miller.

"I retired as the head track and field coach from Oklahoma Christian in the summer of 2015. In all, I was the men's head coach for 36 years and the women's head coach for 29 years. Coach Vaughn was a huge influence on my life and taught me how to be a Christian leader, teacher, and coach."

In the summer of 2015, Oklahoma Christian Alumni Wade Miller was named the new head track coach, becoming only the third person to hold that title in the school's 65 years of operation.

Coach Vaughn stands in front of the track bleachers in his windbreaker and hat. *Courtesy Oklahoma Christian* Aerie.

IT WASN'T VANITY, HIS HEAD WAS COLD

Toward the end of his career, Coach Vaughn, began wearing a toupee. It was not a particularly good toupee, but it accomplished its purpose.

Coach Vaughn lost most of his hair in his early twenties. Even his naval photos show a seriously receding hairline.

The bottom line was that he was subject to getting head colds from the Oklahoma winds sweeping across his bald head. If you think about it, every picture of him outside, and he was outside a lot as a track coach, shows him with some kind of covering on his head.

As he aged and air conditioning became more prevalent and efficient, he often suffered the same results from simply sitting in church or other indoor venues with the cool air blowing across his bare scalp. His practical solution was to get a toupee that he could wear indoors when wearing a hat would not have been acceptable. Basically, it was his "indoor hat". It worked, he liked it, he was not being vain, and he did not care that it was obviously a toupee.

Coach Vaughn adopted the use of a toupee to keep his head warm when in the wind outside or the air conditioning inside. *Courtesy Oklahoma Christian Aerie.*

This change of "style" for Coach Vaughn seemed to cause little concern with his students, athletes, and peers who were more than understanding and who, out of respect for the coach, made little to no comment about it. That was until the night of the "incident".

Fairly late in his career, after he had been wearing the indoor hat for quite some time, he took his track team to Texas for a meet. Everyone, including the coaches and team members had to share a hotel room and it just so happens that one of the freshmen members of the team had family

Head Coach Ray Vaughn with assistant coaches Jeff Bennett and Randy Heath, and the team. *Courtesy Oklahoma Christian* Aerie.

in the area whom he was allowed to have dinner with the first night there. Being a freshman, and as luck would have it, he was assigned to "bunk" with the coach.

Having stayed out later than expected and assuming that Coach Vaughn had already gone to bed, he quietly let himself into the hotel room leaving the lights off and prepared for bed himself. As he slipped into bed he glanced over at the person sound asleep in the other bed and almost had a heart attack, thinking he was in the wrong room, when he saw the bald man asleep nearby. Whether he had never seen a toupee before or whether it actually looked better than everyone thought, it made an interesting tale at breakfast the next morning.

TRACK WAS HIS NAME, BUT BASKETBALL WAS HIS GAME

While he did have some track experience during his career at Harding College, he was a starter and captain of the Harding basketball team. His love of the game was apparent during the four years that he coached basketball at Oklahoma Christian. He not only coached basketball at a number of venues during his life, he continued to play the game as well.

Every Monday, Wednesday, and Friday in the gymnasium, members of the Oklahoma Christian faculty, staff, administration, alumni, students, friends, and anyone else that might have gained knowledge of the game and wanted to play, showed up at lunchtime for what was affectionately, if not too creatively, dubbed "Noon League." After a brief warmup a couple of teams would be chosen, as evenly as possible, and the battle would begin. It was a full court, no referee, call your own fouls, free-for-all governed only by the contestants' sense of fair play, sportsmanship, and Christianity mixed with the underlying fear of revenge should an offense go unrecognized by the original offender.

Coach Vaughn guarding longtime Oklahoma Christian administrator Bobby Rowley during a friendly game of "Noon League" basketball. *Courtesy Oklahoma Christian University* Talon.

In the event more than ten players showed up for Noon League, which often occurred, then participants would simply shift into a rotation, politely called "Cut Throat" which creatively allowed three teams to play on the same court at the same time.

Vaughn played Noon League until the day before he had scheduled brain surgery to remove a malignant brain tumor. Those lucky enough to be in the game with him that day saw him steal the ball from an unsuspecting college student and take it the length of the floor, "coast to coast" for a layup. He was 63 years old. The following day, the surgery was a success in that the brain tumor was removed; however, it left the beloved coach paralyzed on his right side and unable to walk or speak.

A LIFE WELL LIVED
IS CUT SHORT

The first hint of a health problem came sometime in October of 1979 when, while teaching his first aid class, which he loved to do in addition to his duties as athletic director, Coach Vaughn noticed that he was slurring his words as he lectured. An exam revealed a golf ball-sized tumor over his left ear. Following surgery to remove the tumor, Vaughn was treated with radiation and given a prognosis of six months to live. In fact, he lived an additional eleven months before succumbing to the illness on the 13th day of September, 1980, just shy of his 64th birthday.

Coach Vaughn teaching one of his first-aid classes at Oklahoma Christian. *Courtesy Oklahoma Historical Society.*

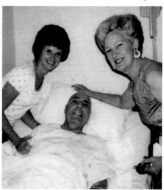

Coach Vaughn following brain surgery to remove a malignant tumor. Flanked by his daughter-in-law, Suzanne Vaughn and his wife, Sue Vaughn.

FIRST MEMBER OF THE OKLAHOMA CHRISTIAN
UNIVERSITY ATHLETIC HALL OF FAME

On February 14, 1991, more than ten years after his death, Raymond L. Vaughn, the beloved coach and athletic director that had given his blood, sweat, and tears to assure the success of the Oklahoma Christian University athletic program became the first admission to the Oklahoma Christian Athletic Hall of Fame. The award was presented posthumously to his widow Sue Vaughn by then athletic director Max Dobson.

During his tenure at Oklahoma Christian University, Vaughn served as the head track coach from 1958 to 1979 and as athletic director from 1958 to 1980. During his career at Oklahoma Christian he served as referee for the prestigious Kansas and Drake Relays, the Big Eight Indoor and Outdoor Championships, and the NAIA National Indoor and Outdoor Championships. He served as a member of the decathlon coaching staff for the United States Olympic team in 1972 and the United States-USSR AAU Indoor Track and Field Dual Meet in Minsk, Russia in 1973.

Vaughn was elected to the NAIA Hall of Fame in 1969, to which he was formally presented for

Director Max Dobson presented Sue Vaughn, widow of Coach Ray Vaughn, with a plaque memorializing him as the first inductee to the Oklahoma Christian University Athletic Hall of Fame. *Courtesy Oklahoma Christian University.*

induction by four-time Olympic Gold Medalist Jesse Owens. He was admitted to the Helms Athletic Hall of Fame in 1976; the Oklahoma Christian University Athletic Hall of Fame in 1991; the Harding University Athletic Hall of Fame in 1992; and the Capitol Hill High School Athletic and Activities Association Hall of Fame in 2006.

In 1969 Coach Raymond Vaughn was presented for induction to the NAIA Athletic Hall of Fame by four-time Olympic Gold Medalist Jesse Owens.

A new all-weather track replaced the old red cinder track at Oklahoma Christian in 1991 and became the new home of the Ray Vaughn Track Classic.

In 1999 Coach Vaughn was among the first class to be inducted into the Oklahoma Christian Master Teacher Hall of Fame. Coach Vaughn (Physical Education) was inducted along with Harold Fletcher (Music) and Raymond Kelcy (Bible).

During his career at Oklahoma Christian, Vaughn coached literally hundreds of athletes, including 60 who were recognized as NAIA All Americans for their individual and team performances.

THE RAY VAUGHN TRACK AND THE RAY VAUGHN TRACK CLASSIC

In 1991, largely with funds provided by the Vaughn family, Oklahoma Christian's 30-year-old track underwent a $150,000 renovation, including the installation of an all-weather, black latex-rubber Omni surface. With the new surface, new features included permanent lane markings, staggers, and a steeplechase water jump. New runways and pits for the long jump and high jump were installed as well as new areas for the field events competition in the shot put, hammer, and discus.

The track at Oklahoma Christian was officially designated as the "Ray Vaughn Track" and dedicated to the coach that founded and developed its athletic program. The plaque dedicating the track to Coach Vaughn reads:

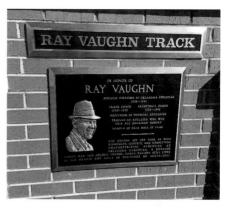

The track at Oklahoma Christian was named the Ray Vaughn Track in honor of its first athletic director and track coach.

> *Ray Vaughn set the tone of high standards, honesty, and competition characterizing athletics at Oklahoma Christian. A devoted family man and church leader, Coach Vaughn still lives in the hearts and souls of thousands he influenced.*

In addition, then head track coach Randy Heath, renamed the OCC Relays the "Ray Vaughn Track Classic" which was hosted by Oklahoma Christian from 1980 to

The Ray Vaughn Track Classic drew crowds for years to the Oklahoma Christian campus. *Courtesy Oklahoma Christian* Aerie.

1985 and from 1991 to 2010 until the running surface became too worn to hold competition.

SUE VAUGHN, A REMARKABLE MEMBER OF
THE FAMILY AS WELL

Sue Vaughn, the devoted wife of Coach Vaughn, was his constant companion and supporter in everything he did. Originally a high school teacher of speech and drama, she too had made the transition to the college level where she taught speech for three years at Oklahoma Christian. She also was instrumental in founding the Oklahoma Christian Women's Association (OCWA) which functioned as a support and fundraising organization for the school.

Sue was also a well-known speaker who often presented devotional studies, Bible lessons, and "book reviews" to various women's groups. Her book reviews would run the gamut from historical to biographical, including the life story of Kingfisher's Sam Walton to the comedic and any book written by Erma Bombeck.

Sue Vaughn, wife of Coach Ray Vaughn. *Courtesy Oklahoma Christian* Aerie.

Perhaps the one thing that brought Sue Vaughn her most accolades and attention however, were the homemade cinnamon rolls that she shared with everyone she came in contact with. They were certainly a staple at "open houses" following home basketball games. They were also coveted additions to other events such as parties, showers, coffees, and the like. Sue would also take a hot pan of cinnamon rolls to anyone who had befriended or provided a service to her. She even sold them for a while in one of Edmond's many delicatessens.

There were also those that got them on a regular basis such as the musicians that accompanied the many productions of Oklahoma City's Lyric Theatre. Sue had season tickets at the Lyric for so long that she finally sat at front row center. The orchestra members knew when "her" night was and looked forward to the fresh cinnamon rolls that she would deliver before the performance. The family has often wondered how they played their instruments with what must have been very sticky fingers after devouring Sue's anticipated gift.

Sue Vaughn was a life-long supporter of her husband and Oklahoma Christian.

Sue Vaughn was so well known for her cinnamon roll recipe that her family purchased a vanity tag for her car that read "CINMROL" and a pan of her well-known delicacy was once requested and auctioned off by the Edmond Chamber of Commerce at their annual fund raiser. When Sue Vaughn passed away at the age of 85, the family printed the recipe for her well known cinnamon rolls in the program of her funeral service so that everyone could continue to enjoy her cinnamon rolls long after she was gone.

Sue Vaughn's Famous Cinnamon Rolls

• ½ to 1 stick butter (or ½ cup Coconut Oil or Crisco)

• ¾ cup raw (or granulated) sugar

• 1 T. salt

• 2 pkgs. regular dry yeast

• 3 cups hot (105 to 110 degrees on candy thermometer) water

• Approximately 5 cups of flour (I like to use bread flour, but

a combination of flours or just All Purpose flour will work fine.

To one cup of the water add the yeast and a pinch of sugar.....
set aside.

Pour 2 cups of the water into large bowl and add ¼ to ½ cup butter or other substitute. Stir in a little (1 or 2 cups) flour, sugar, and salt. Stir all this together, then add "proven" yeast and continue to add flour until it is not sticky. You don't have to knead this, but I keep working it with my hands as I add flour to make sure it is not sticky anymore. You may add more or less than the 5 cups, depending on the humidity in the air. Grease a bowl and place dough in that bowl. I like to turn the oven to 200 degrees, then turn it off once it has reached that temperature. Set the covered bowl in the oven until it rises (about an hour or maybe less). Take the bowl out of the oven and punch down the dough. Let it rest about ten minutes. Then roll it or pat it out fairly thin (1/4 inch thickness) and cover with soft or melted butter or Smart Balance. You may want to divide the dough in half, and use about a half a stick (1/4 cup) for each half. Sprinkle brown sugar and cinnamon generously on the dough, then roll up and cut into about 1 inch slices. Place in a greased pan, spray with PAM and spray wax paper with PAM before you place on top of the rolls. You can leave them out on the counter to rise or do the oven trick again for quick rising. You also can immediately cover them and place in the refrigerator to rise for later. They take a little longer to rise if refrigerated. This is a hot roll recipe without rolling so thin and adding sugar and cinnamon. These can be put out on a Sunday morning and they will have risen enough to bake by lunch time. Yields approximately 30 hot rolls; maybe a few less cinnamon rolls. Also, you can cut them in half, making smaller cinnamon rolls to take to a brunch. Frost rolls with a mixture of powdered sugar and milk, using vanilla, almond or orange flavoring. The thicker the frosting, the better....enjoy.

Love, Sue

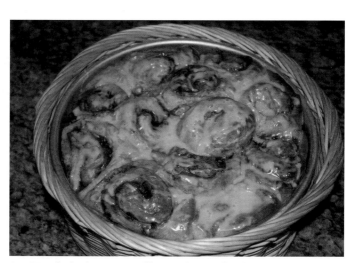

Sue Vaughn's cinnamon rolls were known by those affiliated with Oklahoma Christian and were often served in the Vaughn household.

Olympian Jeff Bennett.

CHAPTER SEVEN
The Best Decathlete Ever, Pound for Pound

Jefferson Taft Bennett was born in Taft, Oklahoma on the 29th day of August, 1948. He was raised in Vinita by his grandmother.

"Jeff," as he is known by everyone, describes his early years as rather uneventful outside of the fact that he was pretty good at his school work and played little league baseball. The excitement in his voice is noticeably different; however, when he describes his first introduction, as a sixth grader, to the sport of track and field. "I was watching the 1960 Olympics and I saw the pole vaulters. Right then and there I decided I wanted to be a pole vaulter. When I could actually go out for track in the 9th grade I told Coach Ron Johnson of the Vinita Hornets what I wanted to do and he let me. I actually ended up pole vaulting, hurdling, and long jumping."

A high school photo of Jeff Bennett in Vinita, Oklahoma.

When he was a sophomore and junior in high school, Jeff finished second in the state track meet in the pole vault and his senior season captured the title in his favorite event while he medaled in both the hurdles and the long jump.

Jeff Bennett at Oklahoma Christian. *Courtesy Oklahoma Christian* Aerie.

Jeff said he never thought about being in the Olympics and that his goal, through track, was to "get out of Vinita" and be successful at something. "If I hadn't gotten a college scholarship then I was going to sign up for the military as a way of getting a start", said Bennett. Ultimately he did both with a stellar career in track and field as well as the Oklahoma Army National Guard.

With a state pole vault title under his belt, along with impressive performances in both the hurdles and long jump, Jeff began to think about a college scholarship. His track coach at Vinita wrote several letters on his behalf to most of the state schools and he received replies from both Oklahoma Baptist University (OBU) and the University of Oklahoma indicating an interest in meeting the budding track star.

Jeff remembers that Saturday in the summer of 1966 when his track coach drove him first to a morning meeting with the track coach at OBU after which they were scheduled to drive to an interview with the OU track coach in Norman. Jeff remembers, "The OBU coach told me that he was trying to build a long distance running program and that he didn't think he would be recruiting field events for the following year, but that he had a friend over at Oklahoma Christian College that might be interested in me. He called Coach Ray Vaughn and Coach Vaughn said he would see me if we would drive over to the school. He gave us directions and we went over there."

Jeff noticed that the school was small, but relatively new. He had a good meeting with Coach Vaughn, who gave him a personal tour of the new Mabee Learning Center on campus. The coach was aware of his high school accomplishments and had already recruited some of the athletes that Jeff competed against in the recent state meets such as high jumper Earl Lewis and sprinter Tom Griffith. When the interview was over Jeff got back into his coach's car to make the next appointment. When his coach got in he told Jeff that Coach Vaughn had told him that if he wanted to attend Oklahoma Christian and run track that he would take care of Jeff's schooling. Jeff said "Well let's just tell him now and we don't even need to go to OU. That was it, we just turned around and went back to Vinita."

When asked how he could make a decision like that so easily Jeff cited the small school feel, the friendly atmosphere, and his impression of Coach Vaughn as a caring and competent mentor that he could trust to do what was in his best interest. Little did he know then that even at such a small school, under the tutelage of Coach Vaughn, he would have the opportunities to compete at the highest levels of competition including the world stage at the 1972 Summer Olympic Games.

That fall Jeff packed his bags and headed to Oklahoma City. His trips back to Vinita from now on would be as a visitor at his grandmother's home.

Jeff described himself while living in Vinita as "quiet and shy". He said, "When I got to OC everybody was new, we were all about the same age. I saw it as a new start. Everyone was very friendly and very nice. I actually came out of my shell. It was just the change of environment that allowed me to do that."

Jeff's freshman year went well and he actually won the 400-meter hurdles in his sophomore season at the NAIA National Meet. However, no one, including Jeff, could have predicted what would happen later that year back at Oklahoma Christian.

YOU NEVER KNOW WHAT TRYING
SOMETHING NEW WILL BRING

In the fall of 1967, Jeff's enthusiasm for his chosen sport of track and field led to a very unorthodox experiment. Jeff remembers, "I loved being at the track so it wasn't unusual for me to show up for practice early. Often, the weight guys would be out there working with the shot and discus and so I would watch what they were doing and give it a try. I was like a sponge, soaking up any experiences I could, trying everything.

"Coach Vaughn saw me out there one day throwing the shot and discus and asked me if I had ever thought about competing in the decathlon. I didn't have to think about that question. The answer was an obvious 'no.' I told him that I didn't have any experience at the decathlon. He said he didn't either. So, we decided to give it a try."

The modern-day decathlon consists of four track events and six field events spread over two days of competition. The first day is comprised of the 100-meter sprint, the long jump, the shot put, high jump, and the 400-meter run. The second day includes the 110-meter hurdles, the discus throw, pole vault, javelin throw, and concludes with the 1,500-meter run.

Jeff Bennett, an unlikely decathlete at 5' 8" and 145 pounds. *Courtesy Oklahoma Christian* Aerie.

"At that time, most decathletes were about 6' 2" tall and weighed between 180 and 200 pounds. I was 5' 8" and 145. I began to practice the ten events which comprise the decathlon and competed in my first competition in the spring of 1968 at the Drake Relays, which is open to all NCAA and NAIA division athletes, finishing in 4th place with 6,950 points. Coach and I discovered that you needed 7,200 points to make the Olympic Decathlon Training Camp and we thought I could improve my performance in the shot put and the 400- meter," said Bennett.

In 1968, with that knowledge in hand, Jeff's second ever outing in decathlon competition netted him a qualifying score in the top twenty decathletes in the nation and a trip to the U.S. Olympic Training Camp to prepare for the 1968 Olympic Games. When that camp concluded, Jeff had finished fifth behind Bill Toomey, Russ Hodge, Rick Sloan, and Jeff Bannister. Toomey won the Olympic Decathlon Gold Medal in Mexico City that year.

Jeff recalled, "That's when the light came on. I thought to myself,

I can make it to the Olympics. I came home and started weight lifting and working with Coach Vaughn doing long runs and sprint work."

Although often included in competition, the decathlon was not recognized as an official national event at the collegiate level until 1969 when it was adopted by the National Association of Intercollegiate Athletics, (NAIA). Jeff's timing could not have been better. That year Jeff won the national NAIA Decathlon title and in 1970, his senior year at Oklahoma Christian, Jeff went on to win the decathlon events at the Texas Relays, the Kansas Relays, and the Drake Relays in consecutive weeks. He then repeated as the NAIA National Decathlon Champion.

In the fall of that year, after graduating from Oklahoma Christian with a degree in education, Jeff accepted a teaching position in the Mid-Del School District and continued to train. Two weeks into his teaching career Jeff was drafted by the United States Army which, based on his athletic accomplishments assigned him to the Special Services Division which placed him on the Army Track Team, thus assuring his continued training and expenses in preparation for the 1972 Olympics to be held in Munich, Germany.

Once on the Army Track Team, a world of opportunities began to present themselves. Later that year he qualified for

After graduating from Oklahoma Christian, Jeff Bennett continued his training as a member of the U.S. Army Track Team. *Courtesy Jeff Bennett.*

and traveled to meets in France, Germany, and Russia. It was Jeff's first time outside the United States and it was clear to Jeff that he was not in Vinita anymore.

In 1971 Jeff competed in the Army Games which took him to Finland. At that point he was consistently finishing among the top ten decathletes in the world.

Having won the decathlon at the 1972 AAU National meet in southern California two weeks prior to the Olympic Trials that summer, Bennett battled Jeff Bannister for the top decathlon position. Bannister ended up with the highest score at the trials with Bennett coming in second. A newcomer to the trials by the name of Bruce Jenner finished in the third position.

Jeff Bennett discussed his preparation for the Olympic Games with Coach Ray Vaughn. *Courtesy Oklahoma Publishing Company.*

Once securely on the 1972 Olympic Team, Bennett spent the next six weeks training fulltime back in Oklahoma. Then, a month before the games were to begin, the team spent a few days in Maine before heading on to Norway to compete in a "warm-up" meet. Two weeks before the games were to begin it was on to Munich and an introduction to the Olympic Village where all athletes were housed.

Coincidently, Jeff's Olympic track coach, from the Army Track Team, was none other than Ralph Higgins, who had twenty years before coached former Oklahoma Olympian J.W. Mashburn at Oklahoma A&M. Coach Vaughn did not participate as a coach in the Munich Olympics; however, supporters of Oklahoma Christian had donated sufficient travel expenses so that both Ray and Sue Vaughn were able to travel to the games to watch Jeff compete.

For the two weeks prior to his event Jeff spent his time doing long runs in the morning, working on his techniques in the afternoons, and lifting weights in the evenings. The day before he was to begin competition he got up and went to breakfast but, as he attempted to return to the Olympic Village he found that the Israeli athletes were not being allowed back into

Media outlets worldwide reported on the attack during the 1972 Olympic Games in Munich, Germany. *Courtesy Oklahoma Hall of Fame.*

their area. While he did not immediately understand why, the rest of the world did as they watched ABC's live broadcasts of what was going on.

In all, eleven Israeli athletes, coaches, and referees and one German police officer were killed during the attack on the Israeli quarters in the Olympic Village. In the pre-dawn hours of September 5, 1972, eight

Palestinian terrorists disguised as Olympic athletes took the Israelis hostage seeking the release of 284 of their imprisoned colleagues. Five of the terrorists were subsequently killed and three captured before the end of the day.

The following day, when the decathlon competition was to have begun, the games were postponed while 3,000 athletes and 80,000 spectators took part in a memorial service in the Olympic Stadium for the slain athletes. There was some discussion as to whether or not the games should continue and the balance of the Israeli athletes and some others did withdraw from competition and leave the area. However, the decision was

made to continue rather than provide the terrorists with any sense of victory. Jeff certainly concurred.

LET THE COMPETITION BEGIN

Jeff's first day of the Olympic Decathlon Competition went exactly as planned. He considered it a good effort and was pleased with his results. However, the second day did not start well.

The first event of the second day of the decathlon is the 110-meter hurdles. Jeff had been running the hurdles since his days at Vinita and was certainly comfortable with the event. However, in his workouts in preparation for the Olympics, when he ran against competition in the hurdles, competitors generally left a vacant lane on each side so as not to come into contact with the athlete running beside them.

That was not the case in the Olympics. With multiple "heats" of runners each lane was filled with a competitor. Jeff's time in the 110-meter hurdles was usually

A television screen shot of Coach Ray Vaughn being interviewed in Germany regarding Jeff Bennett's performance in the decathlon at the Olympic Games. *Courtesy* Capitol Hill Beacon.

around 15.1 seconds; however, on this particular race his arm became entangled with the hurdler beside him slowing him to a finish in 15.58 seconds, almost a second slower than usual. In competition measured in hundredths of a second it does not take much to make the difference between a medal and no medal.

Jeff competed well in the next three events and when it was time for the final event of the competition, the 1,500-meter run, Jeff thought that he was probably in 13th or 14th position, well out of the medals. However, a good race in the 1,500- could move him up considerably in the standings.

Running in the second heat, Jeff reached deep into his training and resolve and won the race resulting in an overall finish of fourth in the world, tops among the American competitors. Bruce Jenner, finished 10th, while Jeff Bannister, the original winner of the Olympic trials, fell during the hurdles and could do no better than 21st. In 1973, famed television and film producer, David Wolper, released "Visions of Eight", one of his many productions, which featured the 1972 Olympic Games, as chronicled through the talent of eight separate directors. One of those directors, Milos Forman, filmed the decathlon, in which you can see Jeff Bennett walking off the Olympic track following the final event. Jeff turns and waves to someone in the crowd. That someone was his college coach, Ray Vaughn, who was at every event during the competition.

To see a clip from "Visions of Eight" featuring Jeff Bennett's competition, entitled Jeff Bennett-Olympic Decathlon 1972, visit vimeo.com/99253150. The video ends with Jeff waving to Coach Vaughn. Vaughn had been in the stands for all of Jeff's events.

A scene from "Visions of Eight" featuring the 1972 Olympic Decathlon competition.

Jeff came home from Munich following the closing ceremonies, retired from the Army one month later, and resumed his teaching career at Del City High School in biology and Earth sciences. And, he continued to train because Jeff was not finished competing and actually planned a return to the 1976 Olympics in Montreal, Canada.

Jeff along with 10th place finisher Bruce Jenner. Jenner would return to the Olympics in 1976 and win gold. *Courtesy Jeff Bennett.*

His fellow teammate, Bruce Jenner, likewise envisioned a return to Olympic competition. Bruce, who lived in Iowa at the time, moved to California in order to train year round. Jenner actually beat Jeff for the first time at the New Zealand Games in 1975, the year before the pair were to compete for one of three decathlon positions on the 1976 U.S. Olympic Track Team.

That next year, Jeff, at the age of 28, was considered a favorite to repeat on the next Olympic Decathlon team. The U.S. Track and Field Trials that year were held in Eugene, Oregon. Unfortunately, just as Jeff Bannister, the favorite in the prior games had gone down with a pulled groin muscle, Jeff Bennett suffered a pulled hamstring while competing in the long jump. Such an injury takes some time to recover from and there was not enough time to do so prior to the games. It was a career ending injury that would cost Jeff his only opportunity to once again compete on the world stage.

Jeff Bennett is injured during the long jump in the Olympic Trials and cannot compete in the 1976 Olympics in Montreal, Canada.

Bruce Jenner did successfully repeat as a U.S. Olympian Decathlete, did successfully compete in the Summer Olympic Games in Montreal, and did win the gold medal.

Jeff said he did not want to stop competing until he had answered all his "what if" questions, such as "what if" I had continued to train and to compete?" He does not look back and has said he has no unanswered questions. He said it was time to go and that he was satisfied. Now, more than 40 years removed from his Olympic competition, Jeff is still happy with his efforts. He is proud that he was chosen to represent his country, content that he competed well, and considers everything that happened to be a great experience.

Bennett freely admits that Saturday in the summer of 1966 when he visited Coach Vaughn at Oklahoma Christian following his high school graduation was one of those life changing moments. Jeff states, "My father was not at home. I was raised by my grandmother. Coach Vaughn was much more than my coach, he was my father figure, my mentor, my financial counselor, and confidant. Sue Vaughn, Coach Vaughn's wife, also was like a mother. She welcomed me into their home and fed me whenever I was there. My experiences at Oklahoma Christian helped me develop physically, mentally, socially, and spiritually."

THE BEST DECATHLETE POUND FOR POUND

In his book, *American Decathletes, A 20th Century Who's Who,* author Frank Zarnowski said "Jeff Bennett remains the only decathlete to compete in every major U.S. Relay venue—Drake, Mount SAC, Penn, Kansas, Florida, and Texas. In fact, he won nine of them. He was nationally ranked for ten consecutive seasons and world ranked three times. He placed in the top four AAU title meets seven times; was second to Jeff Bannister at the 1972 Olympic trials; was the World Military Champion; and made two additional international teams.

"Jeff went out in style in his final career decathlon, the 1977 USA-USSR-Canada team affair in Bloomington, Indiana. Needing every possible point for a win over the favored Soviet team, Jeff won the final event with his fastest time in three seasons, assuring the Americans of a team victory. An athlete like Jeff Bennett comes along only once in a lifetime.

"In his amazing career, Jeff entered 51 meets, finished competition in 46 of them, and won 24 times. He scored over 7,000 points on forty-four occasions and over 8,000 points on four outings. With a personal best score of 8,121 he outranks every other decathlete to ever compete in point production per pound (54.14 points per pound, 8121/150)."

Jeff credits his success to his track coach, Ray Vaughn. He said, "The decathlon was something new in track in the United States. Certainly no one, especially a coach, would look at me at 5' 8" and 145 pounds and think that guy would make a great decathlete. But, Coach Vaughn was an innovator. My work with the weight guys on the track team helped me tremendously with my technique where I was the weakest. On the other hand, my speed, experience in the hurdles, my pole vaulting, and the endurance I had developed under Coach Vaughn gave me an edge in the final 1500- meter event."

While he once looked forward to leaving Vinita to make his way in the world, in one respect Bennett has also returned. A portrait of Jeff, created following his successful return from the 1972 Olympics, hangs in the Vinita High School Gymnasium.

Bennett spent 1970 through 1972 on Active Duty Status in the United States Army. Upon separation from the Army, he joined the National Guard where he enjoyed 31 years of service as a Medical Supply Officer, Military Police Officer, Engineering Officer, and Intelligence Officer. Of that time, he spent 9 months of active duty in Heidelberg, Germany in support of engagements in Bosnia. Jeff retired from the National Guard in 2003 with the rank of Lieutenant Colonel.

A portrait of Jeff Bennett with his favored pole vault pole hangs in the gymnasium of Vinita High School. *Courtesy Jeff Bennett.*

Bennett went on to a successful teaching career in the Mid-Del School District in 1970 and again from 1973 to 1977 where he taught biology; Oklahoma City Public Schools from 1980 to 1991 where he

Lt. Colonel Jeff Bennett. *Courtesy Jeff Bennett.*

Jeff Bennett taught biology in the Mid-Del School District, in addition to other school districts. *Courtesy Oklahoma Christian University* Aerie.

Jeff Bennett as assistant track coach at Oklahoma Christian University. *Courtesy Jeff Bennett.*

taught biology and served as a counselor; and Edmond Public Schools from 1991 to 2001 where he served as a counselor and assistant principal at Central Middle School and at Santa Fe High School. He briefly tried being an agent for the Reserve Life Insurance Company from 1977 to 1980 but soon returned to teaching.

Bennett worked part-time as an assistant track coach with Coach Randy Heath from 1977 through 1984 returning to the same position, which he currently holds, in 1999. In 2003 Bennett became the associate dean of students at his alma mater, Oklahoma Christian University.

Following his appearance in Munich, Jeff became a local print and television personality that was frequently sought after for accounts of his collegiate and Olympic experiences for interviews as well as speaking engagements.

In his *20th Century Christian* article, published in April of 1973, Bennett talked about his Olympic experience, his faith in God, and his college track coach Ray Vaughn.

Jeff Bennett on the cover of *20th Century Christian*.

Jeff Bennett being interviewed by Ray Vaughn, Jr. on WKY-Television. *Courtesy Oklahoma Christian* Aerie.

"I am never alone. Christ is always with me. I believe Christ is in everything, I do," said Jeff Bennett. "I had been raised morally straight, but I was still lost when I came to OC. I received instruction through chapel services and by going to church with my roommate and other friends. I had thought about becoming a Christian. At the beginning of my sophomore year, I realized that everything taught at OC was coming from the Bible. But I was still trying to decide what to do. One night a friend of mine, Gary Butler, came to my room wanting to talk. He explained some things in the Bible that had bothered me. I had always been told that when it was time for me to become a Christian, I would get a feeling inside and know that it was time. Gary explained that God had given me a mind and a will and that I had to decide to do what is right. The next Sunday I was baptized."

In reflecting on his college coach Jeff recalls, "Coach Vaughn lived a Christian life all the time. To have him as my leader has been very encouraging. When we were on the road, Coach Vaughn always made it a point to have devotionals and communion on Sunday morning. This

Jeff Bennett was inducted into the Oklahoma Christian University Athletic Hall of Fame in 1991 by athletic director Max Dobson. *Courtesy Oklahoma Christian University.*

helped me to realize that Christianity is something you live all the time, not just something you put on and take off."

JEFF'S MOST THRILLING EXPERIENCE

When Jeff was asked to recount the most thrilling experience of his life Jeff could have been expected to say his outstanding showing in the Munich Olympics. Instead his response was "It was in my sophomore year that I was baptized. I believe that was the most thrilling experience of my life."

In 1991 Jeff Bennett was one of three original inductees in the Oklahoma Christian University Athletic Hall of Fame. He was inducted along with his longtime coach, mentor, and friend Raymond Vaughn as well as basketball phenome and OC basketball coach Frank Davis.

Bennett has been married to his lovely wife Lisa for more than 30 years. They have two daughters—Lauren Weeks and Raley Bennett. Both daughters live in the Oklahoma City metropolitan area. Lauren is married to Drake Weeks and has two children, Bennett and Maya.

Raymond L. Vaughn (1916-1980)

CHAPTER EIGHT

The Legacy of Coach Ray Vaughn

There are a lot of titles that would aptly describe Raymond Lawson Vaughn. He was an obedient son, a faithful husband, and a loving father and grandfather. He was a farm boy, an athlete, an educator and coach, a mentor, businessman, and friend. In addition, he was funny, spiritual, thoughtful, kind, considerate, benevolent, and all the other qualities that are possessed by a man of God. He was a lifelong member of the church of Christ, serving more than once as a deacon or elder. He could marry you or bury you with the skill of a seasoned evangelist and his soft spoken demeanor and sincerity garnered the respect by all that he came in contact with.

Lifelong coach and educator Raymond Lawson Vaughn. *Courtesy Oklahoma Christian Aerie.*

Growing up as the youngest son of a gospel preacher and educator, that Coach Vaughn experienced an early and repeated exposure to Christian principles and values including many illustrated with references to athletics and competition. Many of those themes found their way into the advice that Coach Vaughn passed on to his students and athletes and are evidenced by the stories fondly shared in this biography of the coach they loved and respected.

A coach is generally thought of as the director of an athlete's training and activities. The actual practice of coaching is the guiding of individuals through a process. Those broad definitions would certainly apply to most coaches of a sport or any other endeavor. However, the great coaches in sports are known for their ability to give direction to the lives of their subject athletes or students both on and off the field of competition.

Sporting News Magazine has published a list of the Top 50 Greatest Coaches of All Time. Names such as UCLA Basketball Coach John Wooden; Chicago Bears Football Coach Vince Lombardi; Phil Jackson of the Los Angeles Lakers; Don Shula of the Miami Dolphins; Red Auerbach of the Boston Celtics; Scotty Bowman of the National Hockey League; Dean Smith, head basketball coach of the North Carolina Tar Heels; Casey Stengel, manager of the New York Yankees; Notre Dame legend Knute Rockne; and Tennessee Woman's Basketball Coach Pat Summitt are a few of those mentioned. The names on that list are immediately recognizable, even to many non-sports followers, due to their reputation not only for success in their respective fields of endeavor, but for the direction they gave their athletes outside the field of competition as well.

Such was the reputation of Coach Ray Vaughn. His interest lay in developing the whole person, not just the athlete. For most of his athletes, the easiest way to learn from their coach was to emulate the way he conducted his life. That is also one of the hardest teaching methods

Lynn McMillon was a miler on one of Oklahoma Christian's early track teams. *Courtesy Oklahoma Christian Aerie.*

because when it comes to your students, they are always watching.

KEEP YOUR EYE ON THE FINISH LINE

Longtime Oklahoma Christian University educator and evangelist Lynn McMillon obtained his undergraduate degree while running as a miler on Coach Vaughn's track team. He recounts a meet held at Central State College, now the University of Central Oklahoma, in Edmond. The track surrounded the old football field in a stadium located just north of the existing Student Union building.

Early one morning as contestants warmed up for their races a heavy fog settled into the area and as runners prepared for the 100-yard dash, an Oklahoma Christian sprinter, concerned about not being able to see the finish line, inquired of Coach Vaughn as to what he should do. Rarely stumped as to an answer, the coach told the young man, "See this red windbreaker that I'm wearing? I'm going to be standing at the end of the

Lynn McMillon became an educator, dean of the Oklahoma Christian College of Biblical Studies, and editor of the *Christian Chronicle. Courtesy Lynn McMillon.*

track in your lane. You'll be able to see me. Don't take your eyes off of this windbreaker and you won't have a problem."

FINISH THE RACE AND PARTICIPATION POINTS

A nephew of Coach Vaughn, Bobby Vaughn was a gospel preacher and former school superintendent. *Courtesy Bobby Vaughn.*

Bobby Vaughn was not only a student at Oklahoma Christian, he was the bus driver for the track team. *Courtesy Oklahoma Christian* Aerie.

Bobby Vaughn, Coach Vaughn's nephew, started college at Central Christian in Bartlesville the year before the school moved to Oklahoma City.

Bobby did not make the move immediately, so when he re-enrolled he was one of the older students and Coach Vaughn assigned him the task of driving the bus for out-of-town track meets. It was on one such occasion that Bobby was called on to "take one for the team."

The meet was well underway when Coach Vaughn approached Bobby in the stands. "Bobby", he said, "in this meet we get participation points for everyone that competes. You're running the half-mile, get changed." Bobby stared back in disbelief and said, "I'm the bus driver." Coach Vaughn was determined, "Look Bobby, you don't have to win, just finish the race. Now go warm up."

Bobby said he found some tennis shoes and sweat pants and finished the race. Oklahoma Christian won the meet and then it was back on the bus so that the half-miler could drive them back to campus. Such was the ingenuity of Raymond Vaughn.

"Coach Vaughn gave me the opportunity to play basketball and baseball in college, which I probably wouldn't have gotten otherwise. He was more than a coach since he was always a Christian example, a good friend, and a supporter in every way," Robert Watson recalled.

Robert Watson retired to Branson, Missouri after retiring from his successful dental career. *Courtesy Robert Watson.*

"Coach Vaughn sacrificed much for Oklahoma Christian with his leaving one of the best high school coaching positions in the state to found OC's athletic programs from the very beginning. Upon graduation from Oklahoma Christian I wanted to go to dental school but was unable to pay for it. Coach Vaughn loaned me the money and forgave the interest when I repaid it. That was totally unexpected by me. I'm sure he did that for others as well but, of course, he never made any mention of those things to anyone.

Robert Watson played both basketball and baseball for Oklahoma Christian. *Courtesy Oklahoma Christian Aerie.*

"Later, Coach Vaughn and his wife Sue became dental patients of mine when I had my practice in Oklahoma City. My office staff always looked forward to Sue's dental appointments and the cinnamon rolls or brownies that she always brought with her." Following retirement, Watson retired to the Branson, Missouri, area.

MORE THAN JUST A COACH

"I want to relay one other strength of Ray Vaughn" said Jim White, one of Coach Vaughn's track athletes from his days at Capitol Hill. "He gave good Godly counsel to young men. I had a very good season of running, losing on only two occasions, and got to run on two state record-setting relay teams [The Sprint Medley Relay and the Two-Mile Relay]. As a result, I had scholarship offers from Oklahoma A & M, Oklahoma University, and Oklahoma Baptist University. I was trying to decide which to accept when Coach Vaughn said to me, 'Whitey, you are a Christian and a Baptist. I believe you should go to OBU.' What good advice! It was while a student at OBU that I became aware that God was calling me to preach. I later served the great Capitol Hill Baptist Church for over 31 years. It was also during those days at OBU that I met and

Jim White, foreground, worked out running track at Oklahoma Baptist University. His girlfriend and later wife, Willa June Mason, held the starter pistol. *Courtesy Jim White.*

fell in love with my wife Willa June Mason."

In remembering Coach Vaughn, Doy Burchel said, "Coach Ray Vaughn started influencing my family by meeting with my parents, Doy T. and Lois Burchel, in the summer of 1960 to recruit me to run track and play basketball at OC. Since OC had no busses or vans in which to travel to games, my parents would take their car to transport the boys to basketball games and track meets.

Jim White spent more than 30 years as pastor of the Capitol Hill Baptist Church. *Courtesy Jim White.*

Coach Vaughn would many times take oranges, apples, and Hershey's Candy Bars for our meals. If we were gone over a weekend, including

Doy Burchel as a young trackman at Oklahoma Christian. *Courtesy Oklahoma Christian* Aerie.

a Sunday, Coach Vaughn would always see that we went to church. Everyone thought my parents were members of the church of Christ because they always attended with the team. Coach Vaughn and his wife, Sue, had the teams over often for meals and cinnamon rolls. My parents were included. As the

Doy and Pat Burchel remember their experiences as students at Oklahoma Christian. *Courtesy Doy and Pat Burchel.*

result of Coach Vaughn and Sue's association, and their influence, I was baptized my senior year at OC and later, my parents were baptized and were faithful members of the church until their deaths."

Pat, Doy's wife, added, "I thank Coach Vaughn for recruiting Doy to come to OC or we would not have met and married."

"Ray Vaughn, visionary, recruiter, coach, mentor and friend; His legacy and his legend. That short, but broad, description, is who Ray Vaughn is to me. I was there in the beginning with him, as he began his career at Oklahoma Christian. What he has done, for those whose lives he touched, is nothing short of amazing....and he did it without any self-serving intention to make himself important, or the center of attention. That's the truth," Frank Davis said in remembering Coach Vaughn.

Frank Davis graduated from Caddo Gap High School in Caddo Gap, Arkansas in 1959. He, along with his brother James, were recruited to play basketball for Central Christian College by Ray Vaughn. Both were leading scorers in the school's first season as a four-year school with a record of 24-2. In his senior year, Frank averaged 26.2 points per game, establishing a record that has remained unbroken since 1963. Upon graduation, Frank was drafted by the NBA's St. Louis Hawks. After failing to make their roster, Coach Vaughn recruited him to return to Central Christian as the men's basketball coach at the age of 22. Davis' 1968 team won the NAIA District Nine Championship. Frank and his wife Judy are retired and live in Edmond near the Oklahoma Christian campus where they first met.

"My brother James and I were recruited by Coach Vaughn, to Oklahoma Christian, in the summer of 1959. He invited us to come for a visit, to explore the possibility of us coming to OC to share in his vision for the new Christian College that had moved down from Bartlesville, Oklahoma. The goal was to transition to a highly successful four-year Christian institution, much like Harding University, Abilene Christian University, Lipscomb University, and maybe someday, Pepperdine University," said Frank.

Frank and James Davis, brothers from Arkansas made basketball history at Oklahoma Christian. *Courtesy Frank Davis.*

"So, I knew him first as a college basketball coach who was searching for talented Christian athletes who were willing to share his dream of making a little bitty, hopeful, new, two-year college, grow into a highly competitive basketball,

Frank Davis, player then coach at Oklahoma Christian, made a name for himself in basketball. *Courtesy Oklahoma Christian Aerie.*

James Davis was a master of the hook shot and likewise contributed heavily to the scoring in the early days of Oklahoma Christian basketball. *Courtesy Oklahoma Christian Aerie.*

track, and baseball power, and one that if his dream should come true, would contribute to Oklahoma Christian's rise to take its rightfully earned place among other colleges and universities. The resulting recognition would say to the world that a Christian university in Oklahoma could compete and win against the more established state universities in our region, and eventually, win against the rest of the nation's universities. He sold that dream to my brother, James, me, and many other athletes from east to west, from north to south. He did that because he believed in his dream, and he believed in the church leaders who were part of bringing the small college to Oklahoma City.

"The thing that appealed to me in his vision for the college, was that he seemed confident and unafraid to say what his dream was. In telling us his vision, it was clear to me that he truly believed in the cause, furthermore, I sensed, even then as an eager teenager, that his goals for the college were

Coach Vaughn talks to his basketball team during a time out. *Courtesy Oklahoma Christian Aerie.*

not for himself and the recognition it might bring; instead, his hope was for the college to be successful in order that the church might be made stronger as a result of the graduates going from Oklahoma Christian into the surrounding communities in every corner of the country. To illustrate what I mean by that, is that he said in a serious convincing manner, that us boys who came and got a degree from a Christian institution of higher learning, that most likely our mate for life would be another Christian, who shared the same values that he spoke to us about. That did it for me. I believed in Coach Ray Vaughn, then and nothing after that ever changed

Coach Vaughn in his office in The Barn, filling out paperwork for some of his lettermen. *Courtesy Oklahoma Christian* Aerie.

my opinion of him. It mattered little that they did not have a gym. I have lifelong friends that came to Oklahoma Christian, responding to the same call he made to them, and in which he believed so confidently.

"I was there with him as a player then later as the basketball coach. During that time Coach Vaughn became a mentor, counselor, and friend to me and hundreds of others. Those other athletes have had much the same experience as I did. Here are names of just a few of the people who came, to share his dream, in early days, that he influenced, in one way or another, as a coach, athletic director, or recruited to Oklahoma Christian...Jeff Bennett, Johnny Admire, Jim Miller, James

Davis, Robert Watson, Lynn McMillon, Randy Heath, Tommy Heath, Tom Hibbitts, James Freed, James Suiter, Max Dobson, Jerry Jobe, Dickie Gray, Juan Jose DeHoyos, Richard Lawson, and many others.

Oklahoma Christian's District Nine Championship team in Kansas City at the National Tournament in 1969. *Courtesy Oklahoma Christian Aerie.*

"One accomplishment, that stands out in my mind, for Ray Vaughn's dream of Oklahoma Christian's athletic program to earn the right to take its place among the best of universities, was the time when our basketball team beat Northeastern State, who was the NAIA's number one rated basketball team, in two out of three playoff games, and won the District Nine Championship. We ended up ranked number four in the nation and seeded fourth in the National Tournament. Ray Vaughn, who had been my mentor and friend, who also had convinced me to come back home to Oklahoma Christian as its basketball coach, had been the most influential person in helping recruit the players on that team."

FIND SOMETHING UNIQUE

Dave Smith, the second of three brothers, was recruited from his home in Florence, Alabama by Coach Davis to play basketball at Oklahoma Christian, but he says Coach Vaughn was instrumental in his decision to come. Smith says, "He took a personal interest in all of his athletes. My father died the first month that I was at OC and the coach took a special personal interest in me. He had a unique way of leadership. People today don't understand the importance of leadership. He made us want to do what was right."

Upon a very successful basketball career and graduation from Oklahoma Christian, Smith embarked upon his own coaching career leading the Oklahoma City Southeast High School Spartans to their first and only state basketball championship in 1976. He then returned as an assistant basketball coach at his alma mater.

Although he had never taken a business class at Oklahoma Christian, Smith remembered something his college mentor had told him about finding something unique. Smith realized that it was difficult on occasions to find suitable trophies and other awards for the many tournaments and other sporting events he led. With that as his motivation, he and his wife Linda established the Midwest Trophy Company, today known as MTM Recognition.

Dave Smith, center of Oklahoma Christian's championship team, dominated the court during his years playing for Coach Davis. *Courtesy Oklahoma Christian* Aerie.

Smith left the coaching ranks and currently oversees 550 employees operating in several different plants around the United States, China and

Mexico. His company has been involved in the production of some of the most widely recognized sporting awards in the world including the Heisman Trophy, Super Bowl and college bowl trophies, rings, and almost everything else you can imagine in both sports and business. Dave has himself become something of a sports icon on the professional bass fishing circuit having won tournaments and awards in competitive fishing circuits around the world.

Dave Smith has achieved success through the founding of Midwest Trophy Company, known today as MTM Recognition. *Courtesy Dave Smith.*

He recalls that his old college athletic director always had dreams of ways to do things better. "They were never about him" says Smith, "they were always about the school that he loved, Oklahoma Christian."

"Being a decathlete meant spending more time with Coach Vaughn than most of my teammates," remembered Gary Hill. The decathlon took place two days before most major track meets. As a result, Coach Vaughn, Jeff Bennett, and myself would usually arrive and compete on Wednesday and Thursday prior to the meet on Friday and Saturday.

Later, during my junior and senior years, it was just the coach and myself. We had many talks together when we were alone. For four years coach always invited me to Wednesday evening worship services. For three

Gary Hill followed Jeff Bennett in the decathlon at Oklahoma Christian. *Courtesy Gary Hill.*

years I turned him down. My senior year I accepted his invitation because I admired the example he set, never demanding, never saying I should attend, never pushing, just inviting. That humble invitation was a great influence on me.

"Throughout my college career at OC my fellow college students worked diligently to convert me to become a Christian. I just wanted to be left alone to train and work toward my degree. While Coach and I talked, I gradually asked questions that I already knew most of the answers to but never thought much about. I became a Christian a year after graduation. Coach Vaughn baptized me.

"Years later I spoke in front of a group of people telling them of the three best decisions I have ever made. My third best decision was to attend Oklahoma Christian. My four years under Coach Vaughn helped guide me in my life.

"My second best decision was asking Marsha Cooper to marry me. I married well above my station in life. Again, Coach Vaughn was instrumental in my life. Marsha went to the coach and asked him about me and my proposal of marriage. He said he saw someone with ordinary talent achieve extraordinary performances during my athletic career. He felt that I had similar traits and characteristics within me. Coach Vaughn married us in a tiny apartment with Jim Neugent as my best man and one of Marsha's girlfriends as a bridesmaid. The girls had little rice packets to open and toss on us after our vows. Coach didn't unwrap his and pelted me right behind my ear. The man had an arm on him. It left a good whelp on me. I still think he did it on purpose. I loved that little ornery streak in him.

"The best decision I ever made was to become a Christian. It made me a better person and a better man. Of course, it has saved my eternal soul. As you can see, Coach Vaughn has been involved in all three of my best decisions. He still influences my life today."

AN OPEN LETTER TO RAY VAUGHN

Dr. Elmo Hall was a tenured professor emeritus of English at Oklahoma Christian. He also was a seasoned evangelist and served the Memorial Road Church of Christ as a Deacon. Another of his loves was OC Athletics and sports in general. He was an ardent team supporter as well as a regular participant in "Noon League" basketball. Dr. Hall was proud of his noon league nickname, which he had rightly earned, and did everything he could to live up to its image. He was known, on the basketball court affectionately as "Elmo the elbow." The following is an open letter that he wrote to Coach Vaughn following his brain surgery and resignation as an elder at the Memorial Road Church of Christ:

Dr. Elmo Hall. *Courtesy Oklahoma Christian* Aerie.

Dear Ray,

The other evening after the basketball game with OBU, I immediately walked to the west end of the court where you and Sue were sitting, patiently waiting my coming to help you to your feet and into your car parked just outside the gym door. As I reached out to pull you onto your feet, I remarked that this is quite a turnabout for you—being helped to your feet by me; in noon league you were used to being pushed to the floor by me. You thought that was funny. But, in a serious vein, I also stated the truth about that being a turnabout. I think of the many young men to whom Raymond Vaughn has provided a helping hand. For more than two decades, you have provided moral, financial, and most important, spiritual support to hundreds of young people. Close to one hundred athletes are now members of the Lord's church directly as a result of your teaching which was reinforced by your daily life.

In addition to your widespread influence on the OCC campus as a coach, you have provided a unique kind of leadership in your role as a bishop of the College church. To be sure, your eldership, as well as your campus ministry, has been quiet—for it to have been otherwise would have denied your nature. Nonetheless, it has been effective; you have offered insights that have always provided me—and your fellow elders I'm certain—with helpful perspectives, and your almost desperate concern for the welfare of this congregation is simply exemplary. I can scarcely remember a conversation in which we did not discuss the state of the College church. Always your attitude was, "What can I do to enhance its spiritual life?"

As a fellow OCC teacher and a deacon serving under your pastorate, I salute you, Ray, for your work's sake. While accepting your resignation from the eldership, I look forward to your modified, but important role as an example of Christian faith and courage with inspires every member of this church.

Your brother in Christ,
Elmo Hall

OCC LOSES A WINNER

By Stafford North

Oklahoma Christian Executive Vice President Stafford North.

When the history of Oklahoma Christian College is written, few people will deserve a more prominent place than Ray Vaughn, who last September- ber lost his year-long fight with cancer but attained his victory in Christ. During the 22 years he served as OCC's athletic director and coach of various sports, the athletic program of the college was a major contributor to the great progress and success which OCC has enjoyed.

During the years the college was in Bartlesville, the school made a start in sports but, with a small student body and no facilities, had not made much of a mark. With the move to Oklahoma City, President James Baird believed that a solid sports program could make a major contribution toward helping OCC achieve its goals. Many a school has failed in such an endeavor. Athletics is sometimes a discredit to either academics or spirituality or both. In other cases it fails because it does not produce enough winners to attract enough attention on or off campus.

Ray Vaughn left his successful work at Capitol Hill High School to join OCC with the determination that athletics at OCC would be a winning program and, at the same time, a real credit to what a Christian college stands for. It was in reaching this goal that he made such a great contribution to OCC.

Ray Vaughn laid a foundation for athletics for those who follow to build on. He did it with two great qualities: integrity and determination. Ray's integrity was absolute. He never broke a rule to keep an athlete eligible, never attracted a student to OCC with false promises, never used anything underhanded to win a victory. Coupled with this, he had a dogged determination which inspired the best in his athletes. He was patient but, never expecting less than the best of himself, never accepted less than their best from others.

Perhaps the greatest memory those closely associated with him have of Ray is his great faith during the last year of his life. As he recognized that he had an illness from which he would not recover, he never wavered in those principles he had lived by. He did everything he could for as long as he could. The integrity and determination he had demonstrated in so many other ways were demonstrated to the ultimate to the end.

A DAUGHTER'S PERSPECTIVE
by DR. LYNN VAUGHN MITCHELL

My dad died when I was 25 years old. That was way too soon. However, in those 25 years he instilled memories to last my lifetime; but, not just memories, more importantly life lessons to carry with me and impart to my children about the way to live, and ultimately the way to die.

Dr. Lynn Mitchell, daughter of Coach Ray Vaughn, has taught at Oklahoma Christian, served as department head at the Oklahoma Health Care Authority, and chief medical director of OU Physicians.

Dad and I shared a lot of memories and I am honored to highlight a few. I like to think we were kindred spirits, sharing a love of animals, outside adventures, humor, sports, faith, and family. Often our time together was spun around one of these themes. Most afternoons following school, Mom would pick me up, grab an Icee at 7-Eleven, and drop me off at OC to be with Dad. I'm sure I was more of a pest than a help, but he would give me small jobs to do in his office, on the track, or in the gym. During the summers, he would let me "attend" class with him and participate in whatever subject was being taught. I became a pretty savvy badminton player during these summer opportunities.

At home, I was usually outside with him, feeding the animals, working in the garden, mowing, whatever chores needed to be done. In his usual quiet way, he would model for me what it took to do a job well, and take responsibility.

One of my favorite memories would have to revolve around his humor. He was not a joke teller, but more a man of quick, dry wit. I would be hard pressed to recall a funny story he told, but I can still hear him pop off with a quip when least expected. I do believe that has to be somewhat genetic, because all of my kids share that same trait.

Dad and I loved our animals. He got me a cow when we first moved to the acreage and from that followed numerous dogs, chickens, bunnies, ducks, and more cows. He seemed most at home with an animal by his side whether that was Tally, Misty, or another member of our constant menagerie.

Coach Vaughn and his constant companion around the house and the track, Tallahassee. *Courtesy Oklahoma Christian Aerie.*

He also was a very savvy businessman. Partnering with family first and then Phil Watson, the family owned laundromats, motels, apartments, restaurants, and my personal favorite, a miniature golf course. He was a hands-on business person and Mom and I spent many hours checking out the welfare of the businesses and occasionally filling in when needed. This provided me with my first paying job as fill-in motel maid.

The other thing my Dad loved, was our Mom. How the two of them found each other still escapes us today. He, an athletic farm boy from western Oklahoma, and she an affable, "big city" girl who preferred the arts; it worked. They loved each other with all their hearts and Mom found herself in more gyms and bleachers than she could count, and she occasionally persuaded Dad to accompany her to a play or two.

So, even though he died way too early, he's here. I see him in my kids when we all sit around a table to play games together. I feel him when I'm outside working in the yard. I hear him when I'm faced with a tough decision or a dilemma. I share his laugh. I miss him, but in so many ways he's still here.

Raymond L. Vaughn, Jr. *Photo by Carl Shortt.*

A SON'S PERSPECTIVE
by RAYMOND L. VAUGHN, JR.

I had Coach Vaughn for the first 32 years of my life. I would have liked to have had more time with him; however, that was not to be. I was blessed with the 6'5" frame of my maternal grandfather and would have liked to have had the athletic abilities of a Jeff Bennett or a Gary Hill, or the coaching savvy of a Randy Heath. Instead I was much more inclined to the attributes of my mother, the drama coach and speech teacher.

During my career in radio and television I decided to enroll in law school. When I told my father of my plans he told me a lawyer joke. My son Lawson, who is also an attorney, is a great deal like him. Serious, soft spoken, thoughtful with a very dry sense of humor. He will quietly listen to the conversation going on around him and then insert his own quip that brings the house down with laughter.

I loved my father deeply but quickly realized, as did he, that I was not an athlete. As far as I can remember that never mattered to him. He demonstrated his love and support in everything I did and certainly *enjoyed the opportunity to score some free legal advice whenever he wanted it or needed it, which was more often than one would think. He had supplemented his income through his coaching career by developing land, building houses and by buying and selling real estate, a skill he picked up working summers while at Harding College. We planned to get more deeply involved in that enterprise upon his retirement from Oklahoma Christian. He died the year before. I wasn't ready for him to go, but in the time that I had him, and my mother, both imprinted upon me the Biblical principles that made them what they were. For that I will be forever grateful.*

What a wonderful blessing it is to be able to live your life doing something that you really enjoy and that benefits others along the way. Such was the life lived by Raymond L. Vaughn. The two greatest commands given to Christians are to "Love the Lord your God with all your heart and with all your soul and with all your mind and with all your strength." The second is this, "Love your Neighbor as Yourself." There is no commandment greater than these. (Mark 12:30, 31).

Coach Vaughn's love of God was evident throughout his life as he not only taught others from the Bible but perhaps even more importantly demonstrated his understanding and commitment to its principles by living his life as an example for all that he came in contact with.

So many people, even today, years after his passing, remember their experiences with Coach Vaughn and continue to direct their lives as he demonstrated and encouraged them. Hebrews 11:4 says that "Abel, by faith, still speaks, even though he is dead." Wouldn't it be a blessing to our families if they could hear us speaking to them of our commitment to God and our faithfulness to his teachings throughout our life and even years after our death? What a meaningful legacy that would be to leave our descendants.

One of my favorite passages in the Bible comes from King Solomon, the wisest man to ever live and to whom God revealed many mysteries. It is a single verse from Ecclesiastes 7:1 containing two principles about this life and life after death. "A good reputation is more valuable than the most expensive perfume. The day one dies is better than the day he is born."

To mortal man both of these statements seem counterintuitive, yet, to those that know and love God they seem in perfect harmony with other Biblical principles. As my time on earth grows shorter I am comforted by Solomon's pronouncement and I look forward to the time that I will see Jesus and be reunited with my earthly family and friends. I plan on getting to know my grandfather better and sharing with my father the wonderful time I had talking to his students and athletes while collecting their wonderful memories and experiences they had with "Coach Vaughn."

APPENDIX

Ray and Suzanne Vaughn
Christi, Lawson, and Clint

Ray Vaughn, Jr. grew up on the south side of Oklahoma City in Capitol Hill. Suzanne was raised in Wichita, Kansas and subsequently relocated to Oklahoma City. They met and married while attending Oklahoma Christian University in 1968. Together they have three children, Christi DeGeare of St. Petersburg, Florida; R. Lawson Vaughn, III of Tulsa, Oklahoma; and, Clint Vaughn of Bixby, Oklahoma.

Ray started his career in radio while in college working at KWHP Radio in Edmond and WKY Radio in Oklahoma City. Upon graduation he moved into television working for KTEN in Ada, Oklahoma; KFDX in Wichita Falls, Texas; KTVK in Phoenix, Arizona, and ultimately WKY-TV back in Oklahoma City.

Suzanne and Ray Vaughn, Jr. *Photo by Rick Buchanan, First Deputy Commissioner, Oklahoma County, District 3.*

While in broadcasting Ray attended law school at Oklahoma City University and started his own law firm, practicing in Edmond for over thirty years. During that time he also served in the Oklahoma House of Representatives, for sixteen years in District 81-Edmond and for the past ten years as the Oklahoma County Commissioner for District 3-Oklahoma County.

Suzanne received her B.S.E. Degree from Oklahoma Christian University and taught school in the Cashion School District until the couple moved to Ada. While raising her family she also substituted in numerous other school districts.

Ray and Suzanne are active members of the Memorial Road Church of Christ where they attend the Cornerstone Bible Class, teach, and work in the prison ministry.

Jay and Christi DeGeare
Jakob and Taylor

Jay and Christi (Vaughn) DeGeare were married in 1992. Jay is a graduate of the United States Military Academy at West Point, N.Y. where he played on the West Point Golf Team. He served his country as an Army Ranger both at home and overseas. Christi is a graduate of Oklahoma Christian University. They have two sons, Jakob and Taylor. They live in St. Petersburg, Florida and are members of the Northwest Church of Christ where Jay is a Deacon and they both teach Bible classes. Jay is a financial manager with Alliance Bernstein and Christi serves as the controller at

the family owned business, VineIT. Jakob has finished his freshman year at Auburn University while Taylor will be a senior at Shorecrest Preparatory School.

Lawson and Erin Vaughn
Greyson, Lydia, and Liam

Lawson and Erin Vaughn were married in 1995. Both are graduates of Oklahoma State University in Stillwater, Oklahoma, where Lawson was a four-year starter on the Cowboy football team. They have three children, Greyson, Lydia, and Liam. They live in Tulsa, Oklahoma and are members of the Park Plaza Church of Christ where they both teach Bible classes. Lawson is an attorney and manages the Cheek Law Firm's Tulsa office. Erin is a legal assistant in the same office. The children attend the Jenks School District and are involved in preparation for college, band, and athletics.

Clint and Sheridan Vaughn
Hudson, Garrett, Austin, and Brooklyn

Clint and Sheridan Vaughn were married in 2001. They have four children, Hudson, Garrett, Austin, and Brooklyn. They live near Bixby, Oklahoma and are members of the Park Plaza Church of Christ where Clint serves as Deacon and they both teach Bible classes. Clint is a business graduate of Oklahoma Christian University where he obtained an MBA. He remains the highest draft pick ever taken from OC by Major

League Baseball. Sheridan graduated from Harding University. Clint and Sheridan own a roofing company by the name of Roofscapes Exteriors of Oklahoma, LLC and a home construction company by the name of Capstone Builders, LLC. The boys attend Bixby Public Schools, while Brooklyn attends Park Plaza Preschool.

Drs. Barry and Lynn Mitchell
Braden and Erin, Barrie Jo, and Brennan

Dr. Lynn (Vaughn) Mitchell is a graduate of Oklahoma Christian University and the OU College of Medicine. Dr. Barry Mitchell is a graduate of Oklahoma State University and the OU College of Medicine. They have three children, Braden, Barrie Jo and Brennan. All three are graduates of Oklahoma Christian University. Braden obtained a Master's Degree from the University of Michigan in Urban Planning and resides in Oklahoma City with his wife Erin. Barrie Jo is currently a student at the OU College of Medicine in Tulsa, and Brennan holds her Master's Degree from OU in Social Work.

Dr. Barry Mitchell is a family physician in Edmond with the OU Physicians Fountain Lake Clinic. Dr. Lynn Mitchell serves as the Chief

Medical Officer and Associate Dean for Clinical Affairs of the OU College of Medicine. They attend the Memorial Road Church of Christ and are involved in missionary work in Tegucigalpa, Honduras.

BIBLIOGRAPHY

NEWSPAPERS & PERIODICALS

20th Century Christian

Capitol Hill Beacon Newspaper

Gospel Advocate, Tribute to Ray Vaughn by Stafford North

Harding College *Bison*

INTERVIEWS

Ballou, Harold "Hal"

Bennett, Jeff

Booth, Wayne,

Burchel, Doy

Burchel, Pat

Davis, Frank

Dodson, Charlotte

Doughty, John

Gray, Richard "Dickie"

Harris, J. Don

Heath, Randy

Herndon, Mike

Hibbitts, Tom

Hill, Gary

Ladd, Don

Mashburn, J. W.

McDonald, Alex

McMillon, Lynn

Mitchell, Kenneth

Mitchell, Lynn

Neugent, Jim

Paas, Dale

Reed, Forrst

Reed, Hubert F. "Hub"

Smith, Dave

Soergel, Dick

Taylor, Frank

Thompson, Ray

Vaughn, Bobby

Watson, Robert

White, Jim

WEBSITES

bleacherreport.com/articles/1277689-the-50-greatest-coaches-of-all-time
dbpedia.org
ibiblio.org/hyperwar/USN/ships/pt/pt-286,html
naia.org
navsource.org/archives/12/05243.htm
navsource.org/archives/12/05284.htm
navsource.org/archives/12/05286.htm
sportingnews.com
vimeo.com/99253150

BOOKS

Aerie Yearbook, Oklahoma Christian College

American Decathletes, A 20th Century Who's Who

Bible, New Testament

Bible, Old Testament

Capitol Hill High School Athletic and Activities Association Record Book

Central Christian College: From Dream to Reality

Chieftain Yearbook, Capitol Hill High School

Cordell's Christian College–A History

History of Washita County, The

Images of America-Washita County

Jubilee

Life on The Line, The Dodson Family

Petit Jean Yearbook, Harding College

Soaring on Wings Like Eagles, A History of Oklahoma Christian University

OTHER SOURCES

U.S. Naval Records of Raymond L. Vaughn

Oklahoma History Center

Harding University Hall of Fame

Elmo Hall, Open Letter to Ray Vaughn

INDEX